Researching Creativity
in Media Industries

Researching Creativity in Media Industries

Mads Møller T. Andersen

LEXINGTON BOOKS
Lanham • Boulder • New York • London

Published by Lexington Books
An imprint of The Rowman & Littlefield Publishing Group, Inc.

4501 Forbes Boulevard, Suite 200, Lanham, Maryland 20706
www.rowman.com

86-90 Paul Street, London EC2A 4NE, United Kingdom

Copyright © 2022 by The Rowman & Littlefield Publishing Group, Inc.

All rights reserved. No part of this book may be reproduced in any form or by any electronic or mechanical means, including information storage and retrieval systems, without written permission from the publisher, except by a reviewer who may quote passages in a review.

British Library Cataloguing in Publication Information Available

Library of Congress Cataloging-in-Publication Data

Names: Andersen, Mads Møller T., 1985– author.
Title: Researching creativity in media industries / Mads Møller T. Andersen.
Description: Lanham : Lexington Books, [2022] | Includes bibliographical references and index. | Summary: "Creative production processes are central to all media industries, and there is a need for more detailed understandings of how these industries facilitate and understand their own creativity. This book offers a theoretical framework to consider how researchers can conduct studies of creativity in different media industries"—Provided by publisher.
Identifiers: LCCN 2022033587 (print) | LCCN 2022033588 (ebook) | ISBN 9781666901696 (cloth) | ISBN 9781666901702 (epub) | ISBN 9781666901719 (paper)
Subjects: LCSH: Mass media—Research—Methodology. | Creative ability—Research—Methodology. | Creative ability—Psychological aspects.
Classification: LCC P91.3 .A57 2022 (print) | LCC P91.3 (ebook) | DDC 302.2072/1—dc23/eng/20220818
LC record available at https://lccn.loc.gov/2022033587
LC ebook record available at https://lccn.loc.gov/2022033588

Contents

Chapter 1: Introduction   1
Chapter 2: Five Traditions in Creativity Research   9
Chapter 3: Media Industry Studies and Key Themes   31
Chapter 4: Production Studies as a Methodological Approach   45
Chapter 5: Challenges When Researching Creativity   53
Chapter 6: Research Design Using the Five Traditions   63
Chapter 7: Case Example: Where Is Creativity in TV Production?   75
Chapter 8: Further Studies of Creativity in Media Industries   83

References   91
Index   105
About the Author   109

Chapter 1

Introduction

Why on earth do we need another book about creativity? A topic like creativity has interested philosophers since the Antiquity and there are countless books written about it. These books are usually either about how you can try to become a more creative person yourself or about how creative we perceive certain people, artists, or organizations to be. In terms of research, most researchers pinpoint one of the first big steps in creativity research to be psychologist J. P. Guilford's speech in 1949. In that speech, he suggested that individuals' ability to be creative depended on certain personality features such as their flair for divergent thinking, which is usually defined as being able to come up with as many ideas or solutions as possible (Guilford 1950). His work, along with several others, inspired a wave of psychological research focused on creativity and we can thank, especially, psychology as a field for these now long-running research efforts that started over 70 years ago.

However, perhaps because of the boundaries between research fields and too little exchange between the humanities and the social sciences, many humanities researchers do not necessarily know about this legacy of creativity research from psychology and other areas of creativity research. In my experience, this is certainly true for most researchers in media studies. Some media researchers are not particularly interested in creativity, which is fine if you ask me. Other researchers in media studies (or within the humanities) are very interested in creative artists, creative industries, or creative work—however, they are quite unaware of the insights from, especially, psychology about creativity. This often means that they are unaware of the existing contributions and discussions but even worse: They tend to forget to *define* what they mean when they say "creativity" or "creative." By looking at the context of what they are saying about creativity, it is possible to identify that they are using an *everyday definition* of the word. In that definition, creativity is usually someone or something influenced by a positive (and somewhat mysterious) force when creating something. Ordinary people can use this understanding and definition as much as they want. In research, however, we need to work with stable concepts.

The biggest problem with the everyday definition of creativity is that it is unclear where the creativity or creative force is coming from. If you think that creativity is a mysterious or divine force that is uncontrollable or only exists inside particular individuals, you risk seeming naive because you express a *romantic understanding* of the concept. If you instead know about some of the insights from, for example, sociocultural psychology with a focus on creativity (e.g., Amabile 1983; Csikszentmihalyi 1988), you know that *evaluations* from people with the power to decide who or what is creative are a very important element in the dynamics of creativity. The romantic understanding is just one example of the assumptions and misconceptions about creativity that are very difficult to debunk.

Watchful readers may have realized by now that I still have not given my own definition of what creativity actually is. Here I will point to chapter 2, which will give a more thorough presentation and discussion of five different understandings of creativity by presenting the framework that I call *five traditions in creativity research*. These traditions represent five different explanations for how creativity works and, in my opinion, you should try to consider if maybe all five of them contain a small part of the bigger explanation and definition of creativity. The five traditions may not all be present and if they are all present, one of them may be more dominant compared to the others. The five traditions that I will present later in depth are (1) the individualist tradition, (2) the sociocultural tradition, (3) the pragmatic tradition, (4) the artistic tradition, and (5) the social constructivist tradition.

Bridging Creativity Research and Media Studies

This is a book for researchers and students with an interest in knowing more about creativity and/or media industries. To be more precise, the book's purpose is to *bring together contributions from the cross-disciplinary field of creativity research and to highlight the insights that can benefit research in media industry studies*. When I am claiming that my fellow media studies scholars tend not to know a lot about creativity research, I do not mean it as a critique of them. I merely base my claims on my own experiences talking to colleagues and attending conferences about media and/or creativity. One explanation for why media studies scholars might be unaware of creativity research has to do with wording and the use of concepts. In what I know about media studies, we often use another kind of vocabulary about creative processes than they do in psychology.

Media studies certainly has a strong tradition for being interested in how media texts and products are created but the words we use to describe that interest are, for instance, *production* and *authorship*. Both literature, art history and film studies have famously discussed authorship and auteur theory at length in order to validate who we as spectators should attribute the primary glory to for making the artwork. That exact discussion does indeed relate to creativity and creative agency. What I will discuss later on in this book about authorship is whether looking for someone (often an individual) to attribute the glory and authorship is still a meaningful way to understand creativity. The same goes for the word production, which also is a key concept for media industry studies. Whether we use the word production or creation to describe these processes around making media content is beside the point—we are probably talking about some of the same dynamics. This means that even though media scholars might not always use the word creativity, theories about creativity could easily inform and supplement the existing tradition of studying media production processes.

A few media scholars have already used creativity theory in media production research and I will point to some of the particular researchers that have been a major inspiration to me. Eva Novrup Redvall has used a range of creativity theories in her dissertation about creativity in scriptwriting, which consists of a production study of the writers in Danish film and television (Redvall 2010, 2014). She draws on the systems model of creativity and the work of psychologist Mihaly Csikszentmihalyi, which undoubtedly has been very influential for researchers from psychology as well as the humanities (Csikszentmihalyi 1988, 1999). In fact, his work is also the key theoretical component in a book on creativity in different kinds of media by Phillip McIntyre. In that book, McIntyre examines different media forms such as radio, journalism, television, film, photography, and music (McIntyre 2012) and in a later anthology, they again apply the systems model of creativity on a variety of case studies (McIntyre, Fulton, and Paton 2016). I single out these contributions because they have creativity as their main focus and use actual theories about creativity (and not authorship or art). However, as the next sections and chapter will show, there are many other ways to approach creativity.

The Connection to Creative Industries

Some readers may be asking themselves: Why has this book not mentioned the *creative industries* yet if it is supposed to be a book about creativity? The first answer is that I see the contributions about creative industries research as very valuable but they tend to come from humanities and cultural studies, which I define as the artistic tradition and therefore only one out of the five traditions that I want to highlight. The second answer is that I am originally a media studies scholar. That means that I prefer the term media industries over the broader term creative industries since I find that media industries have more commonalities and are easier to characterize than the full range of what creative industries might mean (which could include everything from museums to advertising and software engineering).

That being said, the term creative industries seemingly has become more and more commonly used ever since the British government's Department for Culture, Media, and Sport began using it in 1998 to further a political agenda through their "Creative Industries Mapping Documents" (DCMS 1998). The overall response from the research communities in the humanities and particularly from cultural studies scholars has rightly been to scrutinize the political use and possible exploitation of creative industries and their workers (e.g., Banks 2007, 2017; Hesmondhalgh 2013; Hesmondhalgh and Baker 2011; McRobbie 1998, 2002, 2016). In many of these contributions, it is fair to say that the primary objective is to expose and discuss the poor working conditions in creative industries in order to hopefully change this work culture or create political awareness about these issues. I respect and appreciate that objective. However, in accordance with the scope of this particular book, their objective is not necessarily about creativity as a phenomenon in itself. Because of this condition, I label this approach as the artistic tradition and in a later chapter, I will describe how studies of creativity in media industries can use that particular approach from the artistic tradition and from creative industries research to examine, understand, and criticize working conditions in media industries.

Challenging Assumptions about Creativity

Another important objective for this book is to challenge widespread assumptions and everyday misconceptions about how creativity works. I have already covered how the romantic understanding can be problematic because it describes creativity as something mysterious and uncontrollable that maybe only exists inside some gifted geniuses. Here we should ask ourselves if creativity really is mysterious and uncontrollable. What probably makes us think of creativity as mysterious is that we experience how having ideas and being creative can happen in many different ways and that it sometimes does *not* happen even though we have repeated a previously successful approach. Isolating and repeating creativity is often not possible. This makes creativity elusive and this book will argue that it might be fruitful to think that there are many different components in these dynamics surrounding creativity where I suggest the five traditions, even though there are undoubtedly many more ways of approaching creativity.

What also makes creativity confusing is that theories and texts about it disagree about the essentialism of creativity and about whether it actually exists in the world or not. One popular answer is that you can find creativity almost everywhere. An alternative answer is that creativity is a socially constructed phenomenon (e.g., Mockros and Csikszentmihalyi 2014; Westmeyer 1998) where an idea/product receives the label of being creative, which could suggest that the core idea or product is only a small part of the dynamics of creativity and that it does not have the same status without that evaluation. In this regard, it would be useful for the discussion within the broad range of creativity research if more of these contributions were clear about whether they perceive creativity as something that actually exists out in the world or not.

Another long-lived assumption is that creativity is individual and primarily exists inside individuals' minds. This assumption goes back to the early days of creativity research within psychology (eg., Guilford's work) and still exists today. Though many theories about creativity acknowledge that the individual's mentality, education, and general background are important parts, many theories also point to the importance of groups and social contexts in the dynamics of creativity (e.g., John-Steiner 2000; Sawyer 2003; Sawyer and DeZutter 2009). Such theories generally point to how we in a group *collaborate* and *cocreate* ideas and products, which makes it hard to attribute the glory to any particular individual. As later chapters will discuss, this tradition fits well with the collective production processes in several media industries.

Yet another assumption is that creativity is uncontrollable or that you cannot wield any agency over creativity. Some definitely disagree with that assumption, for instance, researchers working with the concept of *constraints*. Many of their research contributions suggest that constraints are important in a creative process and that you can choose to impose even more constraints in order to control or increase your creative output (e.g., Biskjær 2013; Boden 1990; Elster 2000; Kaufman and Sternberg 2010; Stokes 2006; Wolff 1981). This pragmatic perspective is indeed interesting and in direct disagreement with some notions about autonomy, for example, in research from cultural studies and creative industries.

Earlier I mentioned the always-optimistic everyday definition of creativity as this positive force that you should be grateful to experience. In contrast to that assumption, some suggest that creativity can have *negative* effects. Several research contributions follow this line of thought to point out how it can have negative consequences if you strictly focus on promoting creativity (e.g., Bilton 2015; Cropley et al. 2010; Reckwitz 2017; Stephensen 2018). This is something I too have pointed out in some of my own publications where I suggest that expectations for maximum creativity can put quite a lot of pressure on workers and developers in media industries (Andersen 2019b). This critique challenges other understandings of creativity, which I will discuss later in the book.

The Following Chapters

The book as a whole consists of eight chapters that serve various purposes for the researcher who is going to study creativity in media industries. The first part of the book (chapters 1–3) is primarily theoretical. The second part (chapters 4–6) is methodological with instructions and advice for how to study creativity in media industries. Finally, the third part (chapters 7 and 8) discusses television production as an analytical example and points to current gaps in our knowledge about creative processes in media industries.

Chapter 2, "Five Traditions in Creativity Research," is a more thorough theoretical discussion of what I identify as five key research traditions and understandings concerning creativity. The five traditions include the individualist tradition, the sociocultural tradition, the pragmatic tradition, the artistic tradition, and the social constructivist tradition. Throughout the chapter, I will pinpoint some important disagreements between these respective traditions and I will provide a useful model that summarizes the whole chapter in the end.

Chapter 3, "Media Industry Studies and Key Themes," presents some of the important contributions and key concepts in the literature about media industries. The first part points to some central disagreements about autonomy in media industries. The second part discusses the concept "nobody knows" (Caves 2000) and whether it is always true that nobody knows anything about whether cultural or creative products will fail or succeed. The third and last part highlights some useful contributions about idea development and gatekeeping, which can make the abstract and confusing concept of creativity more tangible and usable in an analysis of media industries.

Chapter 4, "Production Studies as a Methodological Approach," discusses the first layer of methodology using a production studies approach. It will explain how you can do a production study of creativity in media industries and why this approach can be particularly fruitful. Learning to do a production study also creates certain challenges because you ultimately need to get close access to the people working in the media industries, which can influence your study in various significant ways.

Chapter 5, "Challenges When Researching Creativity," follows up on the particular methodological challenges that arise when you pick creativity as your topic. Where can you find creativity in the field and can it be "found" at all? How do you empirically document creativity? How do you avoid passing on your own normative evaluations of what creativity is? There really are numerous challenges that you as a creativity researcher need to face. In short, my suggestion is that you shift your focus to how the people you are studying understand the concept and use their understanding and self-reflexivity to shed a light on the complex dynamics surrounding creative processes.

Chapter 6, "Research Design Using the Five Traditions," discusses how you can do research design when you study creativity in media industries. Delimiting your object of study is particularly important as well as being clear about your own understanding of creativity. Each of the five traditions contain certain expectations and valuable instructions for how you can design your study and the purpose of this chapter is to guide the readers and help them with navigating through these issues.

Chapter 7, "Case Example: Where Is Creativity in TV Production?" provides a case example to make the dynamics in creative processes more tangible for the readers. My example is television production and I base it on my experiences researching a Danish television channel (in 2016–2019). In this chapter, I debate where I can go in such a television production process to "see creativity." The example will demonstrate how the processes that produce most media products are often collective, complex, and ambiguous. Production consists of a multitude of underlying subprocesses that all contain elements of so-called creativity. The goal is to show how complex creativity and production is in order to discuss why the key to maximizing creativity is so elusive.

Chapter 8, "Further Studies of Creativity in Media Industries," gathers the main points from the other chapters in a final discussion of what we already know about creativity in order to identify how we should study it in the future. It will synthesize some of the reflections and hypotheses that I have presented throughout the book and present them as more solidified claims. It will also highlight the need for a bigger focus on actual creativity research from media industry scholars. In the end, I suggest that we should move away from using the everyday definition of the concept if we want to gain more knowledge about the many intricate dynamics surrounding creativity.

Chapter 2

Five Traditions in Creativity Research

This chapter will present five traditions in creativity research that respectively understand the concept in five different ways. These divisions are a way of categorizing the fragmented field of creativity research. Academic and theoretical differences can explain why these traditions understand creativity in dissimilar ways but there are also exceptions and commonalities across these traditions. The theories that this chapter will present come from psychology, design studies, creative industries, cultural production/studies, media studies, and media management. By categorizing these theories, I have arrived at the five categories or five traditions, which are:

- The individualist tradition
- The sociocultural tradition
- The pragmatic tradition
- The artistic tradition
- The social constructivist tradition

This categorization of creativity theories is partially inspired by Keith Sawyers categorization (Sawyer 2012) but my five categories should not to be understood as clearly divided or mutually exclusive. At the same time, certain works in creativity research are more difficult to place precisely because they represent more than one of these traditions and understandings. Sawyer's own contributions are a good example of this exact issue because they represent more than one understanding. Consequently, I encourage you to be mindful that there can be more than one understanding of creativity in play at once. There are of course also more than five ways of understanding creativity but when I highlight these five particular traditions, it is to demonstrate how creativity as a theoretical concept has evolved historically and comes from different academic traditions that have similarities and differences. In the context of this book, this chapter naturally works as the literature review, which should give you an accumulated and satisfactory overview of the vast and versatile area of creativity research as well as of the theories that are particularly relevant to the field of media studies.

When you look at when and where the researchers have become interested in the concept of creativity, many point to American psychologists in the 1950s. However, one could argue that researchers in philosophy, theology, literature, and the fine arts started working much earlier with concepts that relate closely to creativity but are not necessarily included in the field of creativity research. The explanation is that they used other concepts such as art, imagination, and authorship but they still discussed many of the same issues and problems, which is why the paragraph about the artistic traditions will cover the relevant and current parts of these discussions.

However, this chapter will take its starting point in psychology and point to the contributions that seem particularly relevant to media studies and media industries. This does not mean that I only look at creativity from the psychologists' perspective, as it is my explicit intention to draw in contributions from several different research areas. A related and yet different understanding of creativity exists in areas of design research and this book will include some of those works to show how it is possible to understand creativity in a pragmatic way as a design process. Additionally, the research areas around creative industries, creative labor, and cultural production have their particular approach to creativity, which focuses on working conditions and exploitation of workers in these so-called creative industries. Furthermore, within each of the previous research areas you can find contributions that express a somewhat positivist belief that you can *find* creativity and isolate, measure, and test it. As a counterweight to that community, there are also works that are more social constructivist and have an interest in creativity as a relative and social phenomenon. Similar to concepts like "success" (e.g., Bakøy, Puijk, and Spicer 2017) and "quality" (e.g., McCabe and Akass 2007) you can regard creativity as a relative concept (as opposed to an absolute). Even though there are all of these different traditions and definitions, this book claims that it is necessary and fruitful to compare results and insights from these different fields that otherwise operate somewhat isolated from and unaware of each other.

In the global West, two particular myths about creativity and genius stand out historically: (A) An *inspirationist* myth where an external force gives the individual divine inspiration and (B) a *romantic* myth where an internal force subconsciously gives the talented genius the inexplicable talent from within (McIntyre 2012, 12ff.; Boden 1990, 12). Another classic distinction, which is useful to describe the research in creativity, is the *individualist* understanding versus the *structuralist* understanding where either individuals or structures receive recognition for making creativity happen. Finally, it is worth highlighting that some researchers point to a multifactor approach that combines several different explanations and gives a diverse, empirical foundation for explaining creativity (e.g., Csikszentmihalyi 1988; Schön 1983; McIntyre 2012). In this context, I primarily subscribe to that multifactor approach, which understands creativity as a phenomenon that can occur in several different ways and is open to interpretation.

Some compare and equate creativity with *innovation*. In order to distinguish between these two concepts, I find it useful to think of innovation as the successful implementation of a creative product in an organization. If we then define creativity as merely the generation of new and useful ideas in any given domain, creativity becomes a necessary criterion (but not the only sufficient criterion) for innovation (Amabile et al. 1996, 1155). This suggests that creativity precedes innovation. However, this book primarily focuses on creativity and not on innovation as a concept since the first body of literature is already very large and lends itself well to themes like idea development and autonomy, which play a significant role in my research thus far. In the following, I will present the five traditions that characterize the research in creativity.

The Individualist Tradition

In 1949, the psychologist J. P. Guilford gives a speech at the annual summit for the American Psychological Association (APA) where he highlights how psychologists until that point have overlooked and neglected creativity as a research area. In his speech, Guilford claims that the creative abilities of individuals must depend on certain personality traits and he equates creativity with the ability to do divergent thinking. He defines divergent thinking quantitatively as the ability to come up with as many ideas or solutions as possible. Consequently, he says that researchers should try to test and measure these abilities much like tests in intelligence research in order to better identify and cultivate the most creative individuals (Guilford 1950).

This demonstrates an *individualist* understanding that supports the myth of the genius and artist that has a naturally given talent at birth. At that time, several other researchers concur and give their definitions of what creativity is (Barron 1955; Stein 1953). These works share many similarities with what has later been labelled the standard definition in psychology that defines creativity using two criteria: (1) originality and (2) usefulness (Runco and Jaeger 2012). This definition implicitly begs the question of how a product is compared to other products and of how usefulness depends on someone's needs in a specific context. Furthermore, other studies have shown that a large number of researchers around the world agree that creativity can be defined as creating novel things that are valued in at least one social setting (Hennessey and Amabile 2010). However, the intention to measure and quantify creativity by testing people's ability for divergent thinking still exists today as a strong tradition within psychology (see Lubart and Besançon 2017; Runco et al. 2010). Yet, in the broad field of creativity research, not everyone agrees that divergent thinking or testing it is always the best way to approach creativity.

Following the same line of thought, many researchers in psychology have used the individual, the genius or intelligence as starting points in their research, among others is the American cognitive psychologist Howard Gardner who has famously written about seven different kinds of intelligence (Gardner 1985). In another book, he has focused on exceptionally creative geniuses like Freud, Einstein, and Picasso (Gardner 1993). Even though his latter book signals a strong interest in extraordinary geniuses and their cognition, it should also be mentioned that Gardner's work does include a sociocultural context and that their genius is primarily recognized within a specific field and domain (a framework that he borrows from Csikszentmihalyi) (Gardner 1993, 88). Additionally, other psychologists have tried to debunk the romantic myth about the creative genius (e.g., Weisberg 1993; Boden 1990) and pointed out how the individualist tradition so far has been unable to explain the uncertainties concerning how creativity precisely connects to genius and intelligence (Sternberg and O'Hara 1998). There are, however, also arguments in favor of the individualist tradition: Søren Harnow Klausen has discussed creativity using a philosophical approach and he argues using an individualist definition of creativity that it is indeed possible to find and isolate creativity as an ability pertaining to few gifted individuals or geniuses. Klausen presents a critique of the sociocultural psychologists for being antirealist and for describing creativity as much too dependent on social systems and social acceptance. Moreover, Klausen points to a fundamental paradox in the concept of creativity by stating that "[i]t is not the concrete creative processes that are mysterious or elusive; it is the very notion of creativity that remains inherently paradoxical. There is something irremediably strange about the idea of simultaneously transgressing the norms while still acting appropriately" (Klausen 2010, 359). His overall message is that a realistic approach to creativity and creative products runs the risk of defining it much too broadly and is therefore in danger of trivializing what a creative product is (Klausen 2010), which could make the concept almost irrelevant in itself.

Furthermore, in 1961, the American creativity researcher Mel Rhodes writes an article about the four P's of creativity that has since become rather influential: (1) person, (2), process, (3) press, and (4) product (Rhodes 1961). He uses these four elements to define creativity and contributes with an easily understandable categorization, which you can apply when studying creativity by focusing on, for example, process. Rhodes however highlights that his intention was to say that all four elements are crucial and necessary even though his categories make more focused studies of just one of these sub-processes possible. Especially his concept of "press," which Rhodes defines as environment or surroundings (Rhodes 1961, 308), is worth noticing since this means that creativity does not happen in a vacuum but that the particular social context, in which creativity takes place, influences the outcome of the creative process. That his theory contains both the individual person and the contextual/cultural press, which also applies to Gardner's book about geniuses, justifies their place at this exact intersection in the chapter. In fact, their works represent parts of both the individualist tradition and the more sociocultural understanding of the concept that I will present now.

The Sociocultural Tradition

During the 1960s, cognitive psychology contributes to a greater focus on identifying and describing the cognitive processes that support creativity. In the following decades, from the 1980s and onwards, social or sociocultural psychology begins to represent a more eclectic field that takes inspirations from, for example, anthropology, sociology, and linguistics (Valsiner and Rosa 2007). This sociocultural tradition has contributions that argue that we should incorporate social dynamics and social interactions when trying to understand creativity. That creativity always takes place in the context of a social environment and also depends on people's motivations, is a particular message in the work of Teresa M. Amabile. In her work, she underlines how creativity research up until then had a focus on personality traits and cognitive abilities but had yet to develop theories with a distinctly social and sociocultural understanding of creativity. Amabile's claim is that many of the previous attempts to test individuals' creativity in reality depended on the evaluator's views and opinions about what is creative and because of this, she suggests that the assessment criterion should be included in the definition of creativity, which most of the definitions at that time did not (Amabile 1983, 359). Her work does, however, also focus quite a lot on individual's motivations (intrinsic or extrinsic), which arguably highlights the individualist aspect. This inclusion of the assessment context has since become central to many other works about creativity within social and sociocultural psychology.

In 1988, the American psychologist Mihaly Csikszentmihalyi writes about systemic conditions for creativity through empirical studies of artists and their environments (Csikszentmihalyi 1988, 1997; Getzels and Csikszentmihalyi 1976). Csikszentmihalyi also argues that the social and historical context should be a part of any study of creativity instead of merely celebrating the individual genius or trying to isolate individuals and their creative products from these systems. He conceptualizes his systemic approach to creativity in this circular model consisting of three related systems that influence and shape the creative product: the domain, the field, and the individual (figure 2.1) (Csikszentmihalyi 1988, 325; 1999, 315).

The *domain* consists of a range of symbolic rules and procedures including knowledge about existing cultural traditions and conventions that the individuals of the domain use—for instance, in mathematics as a specific domain. The *field* is in this case the organizational and social part of the model where peers act as gatekeepers who assess whether individuals' contributions are original and useful. As his example, Csikszentmihalyi mentions: "In the visual arts, the field consists of art teachers, curators of museums, collectors of art, critics and administrators of foundations and government agencies that deal with culture" (Csikszentmihalyi 1997, 28). This means that the field includes, for example, producers, audiences, and intermediaries who all function as gatekeepers to some extent. The third part of the model is the *individual* who draws on their knowledge about the domain as well as their personal background (education, skills, etc.), their motivation and their personality traits in order to produce something original. In the context of media industries, you can think of, for example, television production as a

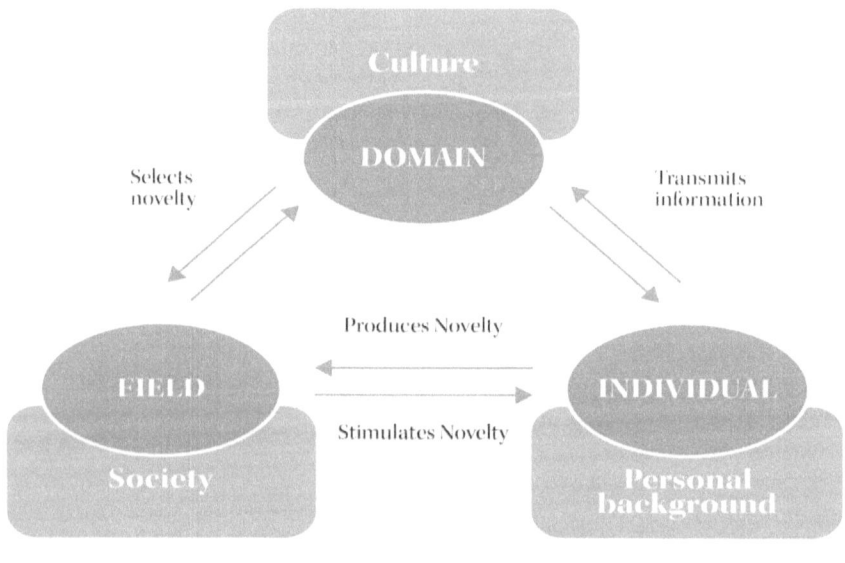

As depicted in Csikszentmihalyi, 1999: 315

Figure 2.1. This circular model, consisting of three related systems, demonstrates their influence and how they shape the creative product: the domain, the field, and the individual. *Figure created by author, adapted from Csikszentmihalyi, 1999, 315.*

specific domain or an industry with a certain set of formal or informal rules and implicit logics while the field consists of the specific group of gatekeepers in organizations and institutions that have influence over the assessment of the individual's efforts.

With his circular and holistic model, Csikszentmihalyi suggests that creativity does not only come from individuals but is very much dependent on contextual systemic structures that facilitate value judgments and knowledge specific to that domain (Csikszentmihalyi 1988, 326). He has added later on that he considers a piece of work to be creative if it has resulted in creative contributions—meaning permanent changes in the domain (Csikszentmihalyi 1997, 27ff.). As opposed to explicitly social constructivist theories of creativity, which will be presented later on, Csikszentmihalyi thus believes that we *can* find and study creativity in a traditional evidence-based sense.

Because of the holistic nature of his system, we could call his work bio-psycho-sociocultural, since it includes both the individual's biology and psychology as well as the sociocultural context of the field and the domain. Even though his systems model stretches across several of the five traditions, I adopt Sawyer's placement of Csikszentmihalyi's work in the sociocultural category (Sawyer 2012). I also choose to place his systems model here because he developed it at a point in time (the 1980s) where the sociocultural tradition was prominent within creativity research.

In the context of this book, I regard Csikszentmihalyi's work as an important source of inspiration as it establishes a strong, context-oriented understanding of creativity. However, I must also admit that I find his model difficult to use in practice. His three-part systems model is generic, can fit any kind of scenario involving creativity and gives credit to both individuals and structures. Yet, it becomes problematic as a kind of self-fulfilling prophecy (in my experience at least) because it fails to open up for deeper discussions or explanations of the dynamics between the three elements. Because it only describes the context for creative processes at a generic macrolevel, it also overlooks the importance of the actual product that is the outcome of the creative process.

As I mentioned in chapter 1, Csikszentmihalyi's work has influenced a few other media scholars with an interest in creativity such as Philip McIntyre and Eva Novrup Redvall. Both of them have used his work to understand media production as a creative process and to argue for a systemic and contextual approach (McIntyre 2012, 209ff.; Redvall 2010). McIntyre, Fulton, and Paton add that each domain's accessibility can have a significant influence on the speed with which these domains implement innovations. In contrast to this, domains with a low accessibility (such as high starting costs or a high skill-level) often create, innovate, and change at a slower pace (McIntyre, Fulton, and Paton 2016, 33). This can indeed apply to media industries like the television industry or the video game industry that require, for example, the right contacts, educations, equipment, distribution channels, and funding at a significant level. The opposite example would be an industry, like podcasting, where the start-up costs are much lower and the accessibility is higher.

Overall, the contributions from Csikszentmihalyi underline how it is important to apply a nuanced, multifactor, and less individualist understanding of creativity. Although they come from different research areas, some note that his theories are reminiscent of Pierre Bourdieu's work on cultural production and whose concepts like habitus, field, and capital have been influential in the humanities and social sciences (Bourdieu 1977, 1990, 1993, 1996). The similarity is that both of them prioritize how contextual structures influence and limit the individual's agency while they also acknowledge the individual's ability for decision-making (McIntyre 2012, 89). In this way, both of them attempt to strike a balance between structures and agents by combining them instead of presenting an either-or. These similarities have also inspired some scholars to include Bourdieu's work in studies of creativity (e.g., Dalton 2004; Toynbee 2000), which readers with an interest in Bourdieu and creativity can check out. In this context of creativity research and the sociocultural tradition, however, I have chosen to focus more on theories with an explicit interest in creativity as concept, which Bourdieu's works essentially do not have.

Additionally, I wish to acknowledge a few other related contributions in recent years such as the works of Vlad Petre Glăveanu (e.g., Glăveanu 2013; Glăveanu 2020), which also highlight the value of employing a sociocultural approach. Another scholar from developmental psychology with an interest in creativity and pedagogical research is Lene Tanggaard. She has advocated for an everyday, universal concept of creativity where she believes that we all show a kind of personal creativity through ordinary actions in our everyday lives. This approach means that we can potentially understand all actions as creative and problem-solving (Tanggaard 2015). Her work is of course in stark contrast to, for example, studies of geniuses and those who analyze creativity as something reserved for incredibly gifted individuals. David Gauntlett is another scholar who has also argued that creativity is in all kinds of everyday actions (Gauntlett 2015) but his background is from cultural and creative industries. My issue with Tanggaard and Gauntlett's everyday approach is that if we insist on the claim that all mundane actions are creative, it trivializes and erodes the concept of creativity. Just as Søren Harnow Klausen has previously pointed out, such an approach runs the risk of making its concept itself irrelevant. Consequently, these contributions seem less significant to the discussions of media industries in the following chapters since the creative processes in these industries generally are embedded in a professional workplace context.

As this section has demonstrated, the sociocultural tradition is long running and has a strong attachment to social psychology. Yet, as Hennessey and Amabile suggest, the field of creativity research in general has indeed expanded in recent decades. At the same time, the number of journals about creativity research has increased and expanded into areas such as neurology, affect/cognition, individual dynamics, group dynamics, organizations, culture/sociology, and, of course, systemic perspectives on creativity (Hennessey and Amabile 2010). This expansion shows the increasing importance of this research area, and in the following section I will discuss how the pragmatic understanding of creativity is also an area of particular interest.

The Pragmatic Tradition

As the previous section showed, several scholars have argued for a move away from the individualist approach and toward a sociocultural approach, which has also meant a greater research focus on collective and group-oriented creativity. This shift is already present in Csikszentmihalyi's contributions but also in the works of Vera John-Steiner (2000), of Paulus and Nijstad (2003) and in a particular article by Keith Sawyer and Stacy DeZutter (2009), which I will use as an example in the following. We can call all of these research efforts *collectivist* but also still rather sociocultural in their outlook on creativity since they focus on group creativity and are highly influenced by social psychology. I have placed them here in between the sociocultural and the pragmatic tradition because they are located exactly in this space between these two traditions and contain elements of both. In Sawyer and DeZutter's article, they characterize creativity as a group phenomenon by videotaping an improvisational theater company's interactions during rehearsals and performances on five nights. During this period, the company changes parts of their show for each night. This leads the authors to suggest that instead of understanding creativity as a mental process inside an individual, we should think of creativity as a distributed and collective process where the originality is rather impossible to attribute to one single individual (Sawyer and DeZutter 2009). This social psychological claim (see also Sawyer 2003) is an effort to debunk the myth about the single-authored creation process and replace it with a more contextual and group-oriented understanding of it. Sawyer and DeZutter's perception of the collective creation process fits to some extent with many media production processes in television, film, radio, gaming, journalism, advertising, and so on since they are mostly collective efforts (see McIntyre 2012; Redvall 2010). This understanding is even interesting to a field like media management studies, which I will describe in detail later. One important reservation about their article is, however, that they examine a creation process where improvisation is central. In my experience, improvisation is a particular kind of process or mode of working that only applies to a few particular situations. When musicians play jazz or when dancers improvise a performance they are working, thinking, and acting in a particular way that I would argue is quite different from how most media industry professionals act. In most media industries, spontaneous improvisation is not exactly the most common way of working, which makes Sawyer and DeZutter's claims more applicable to special cases than to media work in general.

This collectivist understanding has received a great deal of interest when combined with pragmatism in the context of design research. These collectivist research efforts and contributions about group creativity have been an important stepping-stone for some design researchers that have approached the topic of creativity. Keith Sawyer's own work is a noteworthy example of this cross-disciplinary intersection as his research has proved useful in design studies because of his focus on group creativity and distributed processes. A design process is usually also defined as a group process by default and not necessarily an individual process, which makes the contributions from the individualist tradition seem less relevant to design processes. Some design scholars consider a design process to be largely the same as a creative process. Since "creating" and "designing" can have a very similar meaning in the everyday use of these words, the linguistic differences might not be that big. However, in an academic context, we attribute these two words respectively to two different research fields.

One of the most prominent figures in design research, Donald Schön, has delivered his well-known theories about reflective practice and learning in organizations. Schön is interested in practitioners' ability to reflect on their own behavior during a design process (while it is still ongoing), which he calls "reflection-*in*-action." Here he combines the practical dimension of doing, which can sometimes be implicit or tacit (see also Polanyi 1967 about tacit knowledge), with thinking and reflecting on the practical dimension. He also mentions "reflection-*on*-action" that takes place after the process has ended and, in both cases, the purpose is to learn from how the process went (Schön 1983, 280). In this way, Schön defines design as a reflexive conversation with the materials in a design situation (Schön 1992) and his definition therefore highlights *the ability to reflect* and *the use of materials.* The purpose behind the designers' actions here is of course to streamline the design process and make it more efficient. Another design researcher, Charles Owen, describes design as "the creation process through which we employ tools and language to invent artifacts and institutions. As society has evolved, so has our ability to design" (Owen 1993, 2). In contrast to Schön, Owen's definition points to *the invention of artifacts or products* and to *the use of tools* as essential elements in design. These focus points highlight the design tradition's key interest in the final product, which will be the most important result from the design process and of course has to meet the expectations from customers and users in terms of functionality, usability, and customer satisfaction. That the product, the customer, and the market relevance play a significant role separates design research to some extent from, for instance, psychology and the research in creative industries. The focus on tools that Charles Owen and other design scholars have can also lead to a preference for using prescriptive models, process-oriented software, and practical exercises as pragmatic tools to control and enhance the process. This means that designers can have the self-understanding that they have an active role and are able to control creative processes by actively choosing, for example, to use an exercise to further the process. This can make them feel a high degree of agency and explains why scholars and practitioners from this pragmatic and collectivist tradition do not necessarily think of creativity as particularly mysterious but as a phenomenon that you can control or navigate through.

These general features in particular areas of design research are similar to the pragmatic philosophy that we find in the work of John Dewey (1916, 1934/1958). Therefore, the dominant philosophical perspective in design research is often pragmatism (Dalsgaard 2014). There is also a fundamental difference between this pragmatic and practice-oriented tradition and several of the other traditions because design researchers sometimes *participate actively in creating products in cooperation with their informants* (e.g., Koskinen 2011; Vaughan 2017; Cross 2006). Because design researchers can also be designers themselves, it gives them the opportunity to participate actively in the construction of a design product while they afterward can use their first-hand knowledge about the process in their research. This practice sets them apart from the observing role that some researchers from the humanities or social sciences can have in their fieldwork—including myself.

Researchers from both psychology and design with an interest in creativity sometimes use the concept of *constraints*, which we can describe as the conditions that can affect what is possible in a specific creative process. Constraints have a double role where they can both limit and enhance since they are both an obstacle and a resource. This interpretation of the concept can be found in the work of several different scholars like Margaret A. Boden (1990, 82ff.), Jon Elster (2000), and in Patricia D. Stokes's work on constraints and creative problem-solving where she categorizes a number of constraints in pairs. Stokes also highlights how so-called creative experts are more inclined to actively use constraints than their less experienced colleagues (Stokes 2006). A particularly interesting category contains the self-imposed constraints, where designers voluntarily introduce constraints or dogmas that they believe will benefit the process (Biskjær 2013). Even though Jon Elster attempts to do so, it is very difficult if not impossible to make an exhaustive typology of *all* the constraints that can affect such processes (Biskjær and Halskov 2014,

28; Elster 2000). This circumstance naturally creates problems for what you can do with constraints as a concept since you will never be able to describe every single constraint in a particular situation. Instead, Biskjær and Halskov suggest that we can focus on "decisive constraints" and radical decision-making, which is when designers drastically limit their own number of available solutions by imposing constraints on themselves (Biskjær and Halskov 2014, 55). Such an approach to constraints as a concept then highlights how creative practitioners can take an active role and exhibit conscious decision-making and self-limitation in order to try to achieve radical creativity or major breakthroughs.

Even though this book will not encourage you to use constraints as an analytical tool, the described understanding of constraints and their double role as both an obstacle and a resource will be very relevant in the later discussions and disagreements about, for example, poor working conditions in media industries. In the pragmatic tradition and from a design studies perspective, less fortunate working conditions such as a small budget or a short-term contract can both limit and further your creative output. This consideration is sometimes a bit provoking to some researchers but nonetheless a common condition in many media industries today—and we will return to this key discussion around autonomy in creative work later on in chapter 3.

In order to discuss the pragmatic design researchers' focus on processes, tools and products, we could dare to ask, Why is it at all important for researchers to develop tools and products? This is where the pragmatic tradition encourages a way of thinking and working where the instinctive response to a malfunctioning tool or product is to merely replace it with another tool or product. Instead, we could also use such situations to discuss why it always is necessary to construct a tool or product. Or in the case of research products: Why do we need another model? In psychology or in the humanities, a tool or product is not the output of all research processes. However, this is the knee jerk reaction in the pragmatic tradition's way of working since it focuses on optimizing the tool or product. It is, in some ways, also this tradition's strength as working with making products allows designers to reflect on their own actions and be present, aware, and active in controlling creative processes and to learn from their mistakes.

Parallel to how design researchers work, the research in media management employs a quite similar approach. Media management research works with topics such as management, leadership or entrepreneurship in media firms and relates creativity to such topics. Researchers like Howard Davis and Richard Scase (2000), Chris Bilton (Bilton 2007; Bilton and Cummings 2010), and Lucy Küng (2008) have all described how managers can manage creativity and the potential difference between "suits" and "creatives" in organizational work as Bilton calls it. These contributions also understand creativity in the pragmatic sense and that creativity is a question of using the right management strategy in order to streamline processes and maximize outputs. In this context, Lucy Küng defines creativity as a "critical strategic resource" (Küng 2008, 145) and in today's highly competitive media industries, it is easy to see why creativity as a concept receives a lot of attention from media organizations who often want to brand themselves as buzzing with creativity. Media management literature about creativity lends itself well to managers and organizations with these interests even though the downside can be that they sometimes disregard the workers' perspective.

In summary, the pragmatic tradition consists of a mixed field of contributions from both psychology, design and media management that all have the same interests in common. They often want to optimize creative and collective work processes and recommend best practices using tools, models, and products, which can be sensible enough as long as the researchers remember to have critical reflections about the potential downsides to this approach. Critics of this pragmatic and functionalist approach argue that such research is merely helping commercial and capitalist companies to colonize the concept of creativity so that it can be used to justify financial gains or questionable working conditions (see this critique in Deuze 2019). Another objection could be that this tradition's intense focus on group processes makes it easy to forget the individual perspectives in the process and how each individual is a person with particular traits (who they are, what they are feeling and how individual actions shape creative processes). The nature of these critiques logically lead us to the next tradition, which is the artistic tradition.

The Artistic Tradition

The fourth tradition that I will characterize now comes from research fields such as cultural studies, cultural production, and so-called creative industry studies. Compared to the three previous traditions, the artistic tradition consists of a more fragmented and less uniform collection of contributions from many different research fields within the humanities. Some of the research that I will present is maybe not always that useful as analytical tools but still crucial in order to understand historically where the perception of creativity in the humanities comes from. What they all have in common is that they are interested in discussing whom we should give credit to in the creative process and who the creator is. In this tradition, the researchers often conflate the respective concepts of creativity and art, as they perceive these two concepts as almost identical. In, for instance, Howard Becker's classic book *Art Worlds* (1982), he does not directly write about creativity but he does describe the art world, how the artist as a profession has an exclusive reputation and how society apparently allows artists to work more freely outside traditional norms (Becker 1982). Becker mentions the myth of the artist that both the art worlds and societies in general accept, which is "that the making of art requires special talents, gifts, or abilities, which few have" (Becker 1982, 14). This image of this gifted artist is a rather narrow and slightly old-fashioned understanding that is somewhat similar to the individualist tradition's simplified focus on a single individual.

If we then look at literary studies, there are classic discussions around authorship, the creation of texts, and the author's role, which shape how research from literary studies understand the concept of creativity. In this context, Roland Barthes's famous announcement of the "death of the author" (*La mort de l'Author*, 1967) is relevant where Barthes—in a feud with traditional literary studies—removes much of the creative glory and explanatory power from the author and his or her intentions and gives it to the readers and their interpretation of the work (Barthes 2004). Similarly, Michel Foucault discusses in his essay what an author is (*Qu'est-ce qu'un Auteur*, 1969) and defines the author as a discursive and ideological entity, which we can use in texts to give them a particular meaning as opposed to, for exmaple, anonymous texts (Foucault 2015).

These discussions of authorship and the process of creation in cultural production are also present in film studies. The film critic and new wave director François Truffaut and the Parisian journal *Cahiers du Cinema* played a key part in introducing the auteur concept in the 1950s. This discussion was later revived by the American film critic Andrew Sarris, who in his theory creates a number of particular requirements that film directors should live up to before he can consider them for his pantheon where only the greatest film auteurs are included (Sarris 1963). Peter Wollen later discusses Sarris's semi-elitist approach and instead offers a more structuralist approach to film directors as auteurs focusing on contradictions and structures in their work and not only on their personalities (Wollen 1972). Janet Staiger has also contributed with a historical overview of authorship and mentions seven different approaches to the concept. She explains how the general understanding of authorship (also in literature and cultural studies) has varied. It has moved from the classic celebration of the author to understanding the author as merely a small part of a much larger system of production, as a theoretical construction in the readers' minds, as a discursive entity or even as a subversive and self-conscious activist (Staiger 2003). These efforts all demonstrate how the discussion of creativity in film studies has played out even though this discussion of authorship has often resulted in giving most of the attention to the film directors as creative individuals instead of giving it to other members of the production team.

We can now see that all of these discussions of authorship in literature, art, and film studies provide a multitude of approaches including romantic, formalist, poststructuralist, and feminist approaches. This multitude of approaches is why I describe the artistic tradition as more fragmented but also as generally fascinated with the auteurs that we give credit to in literature, art, or film. Furthermore, as Vicky Mayer points out, there is a tendency to forget the below-the-line workers in film and television production even though they contribute immensely to the collective production process. As a consequence, film and television cultures in general still tend to mainly celebrate above-the-line employees like actors, directors, and scriptwriters as auteurs (Mayer 2011). Just look at movie posters and notice what names and roles they write in big print. Chris Bilton also explains this overall focus on big names in cultural production. He writes that individual stars can have tremendous brand value and that it is much easier to communicate that we should give most of the credit to one person for the creation of an artwork instead of explaining the intricate details of the actual, collective creation process (Bilton 2013, 128–29). These communicative difficulties are a general challenge since promotion efforts rarely describe or represent the actual and complex creative processes that came before.

As mentioned in the beginning of this chapter, there is a particular research tradition in *creative industries*. This tradition is more visible in the UK than in the rest of Europe and the reason is that the British Labour government around the millennium made a number of new policies in this area. In 1998, the Department for Culture, Media and Sport (DCMS) introduced the concept of creative industries as a specific sector and a political and economic focus area that had a potential for growth. With their neoliberal agenda, they defined this sector as containing a long list of professions including: "music, performing arts, publishing software, TV and radio, designer fashion, advertising, arts and antiques, crafts, design, architecture, interactive leisure software" (DCMS 1998). Since the introduction of that policy, the creative industries have been widely discussed in a number of research contributions that wanted to challenge this neoliberal political agenda by describing problematic working conditions, class divides, and a general lack of diversity (Schlesinger 2007). However, it is worth noticing that this list of professions is so long and diverse that we could argue that the organizational cultures and working conditions in the respective areas of architecture, radio, and software production are probably rather different. On the other hand, there can be some common features between some of these professions—but the question is whether it at all makes sense to talk about creative industries as *one* particular and uniform sector when these industries are so many and so diverse. For further delimitation of the creative industries you can consult the overview made by Candace Jones, Mark Lorenzen, and Jonathan Sapsed in their publication about this exact subject where they compare several different definitions and lists of various industries (Jones, Lorenzen, and Sapsed 2015).

The British cultural studies researcher Angela McRobbie has written much about the creative industries and often with a focus on the fashion industry (McRobbie 1998) in order to characterize the developments that this industry has undergone. She points to the expansion of the unsure, flexible, and flamboyant working life that previously mostly applied to professions like writers, artists, directors, and fashion designers and that now is true for many other professions in the creative industries today where precarious and underpaid working conditions are common. McRobbie worries that this neoliberal tendency lures young workers into the creative industries with the illusion that they will be "liberated" from permanent employment leading them to become more individualized and live uncertain working lives. She writes that "[t]hrough the profusion of profiles and interviews with hairdressers, cooks, artists, and fashion designers, the public (especially young people) are presented with endless accounts of the seemingly inherent rewards of creative labour. [. . .] It is certainly not the case that now, in post-industrial Britain, people genuinely have the chance to fulfill their creative dreams" (McRobbie 2002, 517). As this quote demonstrates, McRobbie does not buy the industries' narrative about how you can fulfill your dreams by having a liberated career in the creative industries. However, she is not very clear about how she defines creativity when she mentions creative labor and her use of the concept is probably just a reference to these particular industries instead of an interest in the actual concept itself. Consequently, her works have a tendency to see creativity as an unproblematic given and promotes an outdated, romantic perception of the concept. Her primary point is nonetheless valuable because she underlines how words like creativity and innovation are often just buzzwords used in these industries to create confusion about the actual working conditions (McRobbie 2016).

Another British scholar in this tradition, Mark Banks, has a similarly critical perspective in his discussions of the creative industries. He, however, points out that young people's choice to work in these industries despite the working conditions might actually be an ideological and conscious choice to disregard the capitalist notion of necessarily wanting a high salary (Banks 2007). In his latest book, Banks uses the work as a professional musician as an example and describes it as extremely precarious, poorly paid, and divided into many little gigs, which is still of value to the musician because he loves his music. Banks describes this distinction with two categories: *internal* and *external goods* (Banks 2017, 44). The internal goods consist of the joy you achieve from doing the work (e.g., if playing jazz music makes you happy) and the ability to appreciate the particular skills that this work requires. For instance, you may need a certain insight and knowledge about chess to be able to appreciate and recognize the talents of a skilled chess player. In contrast, the external goods can be money, prestige, and other things that you in principle can achieve though doing many kinds of work. Concerning jazz music, Banks states, in his analysis, that producers and consumers are interested in jazz for the sake of jazz and not because of external goods since they listen to jazz to satisfy their own interest in the music (Banks 2017, 48–51). While Banks's statements here do point to problematic working conditions, he simultaneously highlights the internal goods and the personal fulfillment that workers in creative industries experience, which indeed may explain some of their career choices. His concepts of internal and external goods are of course reminiscent of Amabile's concepts of intrinsic and extrinsic motivation (Amabile 1996). These assumptions about how people are motivated by strong feelings of internal desire to do certain tasks have however also been criticized for being somewhat romantic assumptions (see Eisenberger and Shanock 2003).

Another critical voice in these discussions is David Hesmondhalgh whose contributions often use the term "cultural industries" and similarly discuss these industries' working conditions. He describes how the products of the cultural industries (e.g., news, documentaries, books, movies, TV shows, comics, music, games, etc.) influence our understanding of and knowledge about the world and that we must regard these industries and their products as complex, ambivalent, and contested (Hesmondhalgh 2019). In contrast to many of the other scholars in this tradition, Hesmondhalgh actually defines his concept of creativity, which he calls symbolic creativity and regards as "a particular kind of creativity [. . .] the manipulation of symbols for the purposes of entertainment, information and perhaps even enlightenment" (Hesmondhalgh 2019, 9). He explains that when he mentions creativity or creative work, he is referring to all equal types of work in the cultural industries. Yet, he later contradicts himself by emphasizing that only certain kinds of creative work are good while bad or banal work is done in the interest of commercialism or serving those in power (Hesmondhalgh 2019, 10). Due to his distinction between creativity and commerce, it is fair to say that he too uses a particularly normative, narrow, and possibly romantic concept of creativity that only includes artistic and noncommercial workers and products. The self-contradiction in his definition here is that he argues both for and against the romantic glorification of creative work and artists. He goes on to state that autonomy is a good condition for creative work while he, in this context, defines control as bad for the creative work (Hesmondhalgh 2019, 337–38). As the end of this section will point out, this is a fundamental misconception about creativity, which we can also find in the work of Bill Ryan (1991) that predates and has inspired Hesmondhalgh's work among others.

In addition, Hesmondhalgh characterizes the workforce and the conditions in the cultural industries: Most employees have several jobs at once, are hired as freelancers or on short-term contracts, have uncertain career futures, have poor or unequal salaries, and the workforce is rather young but steadily growing in numbers (Hesmondhalgh 2019, 351). We can find similar statements in the works of a number of British and American scholars within this tradition in the area of "creative labor studies" (e.g., Gill and Pratt 2008; Hesmondhalgh and Baker 2011; Lee 2012; Ross 2008; Ursell 2000; Zoellner 2015; Mayer 2011; Schlesinger 2010). Works in this area often discuss the creative industries as a capitalist instrument or as exploiting workers and sees these industries in a more or less critical or Marxist perspective. Some of the works also highlight some important inequalities in terms of gender, race, and minority backgrounds (for instance BAME, "black, Asian and minority ethnic") in these industries (Conor, Gill, and Taylor 2015; Saha 2017). However, many of these contributions concerning creative labor are generally not interested in defining or discussing how we can understand creativity but only how we can expose the industries' poor working conditions.

Due to their interest in working conditions, these contributions (here represented by the works of McRobbie, Banks, and Hesmondhalgh) typically use the labels "creativity" and "creative" in the widest possible sense to describe work and workers in the industries mentioned by the British government as a political focus area. Their work is inherently political as well as normative and usually voices a critique of the government's efforts to instrumentalize creative industries. In opposition to the works from psychology and design about creativity (which the contributions in the artistic tradition are apparently unaware of), the research in creative industries is much more focused on how cultural products can influence society and on the harmful impact that these industries have on young workers. Since the works here rarely discuss how we should study or define creativity, we must assume that they generally use the everyday definition of the concept as someone influenced by a positive force when creating something. This is why they often still maintain the romantic and naïve notion that creativity should just be "set free," which is in direct opposition to the insights from the pragmatic tradition about, for example, self-imposing constraints to further a creative process.

The difference between the artistic and the pragmatic tradition is inherently ideological and rooted in the clash between Marxist and capitalist ideas about whether the purpose of research into cultural production is to liberate workers or optimize products and incomes. Still, the important and fruitful insight from the artistic tradition is undoubtedly both the discussion of who the authorship in literature, art, and film belongs to and the politically vital awareness of the precarious working conditions in creative industries.

The Social Constructivist Tradition

As this fifth and final section of the chapter will demonstrate, there is another group of scholars who use an inherently social constructivist approach to creativity. Still, this is probably the smallest of the five traditions in this book.

Here it is worth mentioning the works of Stephanie Taylor that stand out because of her background in social psychology, and which express a psychological interest in the identity and self-perception of creative workers. We can thereby situate Taylor's work in the intersection between social psychology and creative industries. Taylor has pointed out that McRobbie probably overlooks the condition that young workers are, in fact, well-informed about the challenges of working in these industries and that they make a conscious choice to pursue what they themselves describe as a calling and a vocation (Taylor 2012, 44). Through her interviews with former students from art, fashion, photography, product design, and animation from British art schools, she compiles a more ambivalent image of how young workers are not powerless and how they and the creative industries they go into form their careers and professional identities. Her informants are not that concerned about the precarious working conditions but much more positive about the flexibility in their working lives while they focus on their future and believe that the big break could be right around the corner. This narrative is more ambivalent and multisided, not unlike the internal goods that Banks's described using passionate jazz musicians. However, she does highlight to how a strong passion and love for the work in these industries can have an emotional cost because of the strong connection to oneself: "the personalised nature of the work, creating out of 'yourself' or doing 'your own work' means that creative work involves the worker giving of her or himself. This is the emotional labour which has also been noted as a feature of contemporary creative work" (Taylor 2012, 54).

In other works, Taylor has used a narrative and discursive approach to the concept of creativity and defined creativity as a social phenomenon that depends on the social and collective context. This means that creativity can be a part of social negotiations where several competing and even contradictory definitions of the concept can be in play at the same time. Thus, she describes how there can be many different discourses about creativity used by both scholars and industry professionals where she tries to debunk the search for creativity (Taylor 2013, 180). When she uses this social constructivist approach, she is not normatively searching for what is creative and what is not because she instead is interested in the workers' professional self-perceptions as creatives or noncreatives—as she does in her book with Karen Littleton (Taylor and Littleton 2012). Taylor's contributions demonstrate how a combination of several traditions in creativity research can be fruitful: She combines the critical and artistic tradition from the humanities focused on working conditions combined with a sociocultural tradition and social constructivist understanding of how identities are shaped. This means that she can provide multisided explanations for how and why informants sometimes have several competing definitions of creativity in play at the same time. These works from Taylor stand out in this way from several other humanities scholars because she abandons the idea of finding creativity and the widespread myth that creativity should just be "set free." However, in two recent anthologies with Susan Luckman, their focus is primarily on how workers find new pathways into creative working lives and how they try to adapt to the new normal created by creative industries' precarious working conditions (Luckman and Taylor 2018; Taylor and Luckman 2020).

This approach within the social constructivist tradition does not encourage us to isolate "creativity" or examine it as a stroke of genius but regards it as a relative term or as some sort of floating signifier (Laclau and Mouffe 2001). In a similar way, another scholar called Hans Westmeyer has argued for a social constructivist approach to creativity with the argument that creativity is incredibly dependent on assessments and evaluations. He states that it is not until the evaluation that a product gets the label of being "creative" and that we therefore cannot exclusively describe creativity as an ability that people have or as particular features that products have (Westmeyer 1998, 14).

That creativity is a relative term is also something that the Australian researcher Stuart Cunningham has asserted in an article about how various political entities use and interpret the term "creative industries" in many different ways—like a Rorschach inkblot (Cunningham 2009). All these relative understandings of the creativity concept are not unlike Csikszentmihalyi's statement about how creativity is exactly a matter of contextual factors and assessments also from audiences and that "what we call creativity is a phenomenon that is constructed through an interaction between producer and audience" (Csikszentmihalyi 1999, 314). Here we find the idea of how creative products are dynamic and that what particular societies or organizations consider as creative might change over time.

The difference between the sociocultural and the social constructivist tradition in this regard is that the contributions in the former tradition mostly believe that we *can* find and detect creativity as a phenomenon while a hard social constructivist would disagree. The helpful aspect of this tradition is that it allows you to shift your focus from normatively searching for creativity and instead focus on the informants own narratives and perceptions of what creativity is. I have used this approach in a previous publication (Andersen 2017) but I currently try to combine all five traditions when I study creative processes in order to consider which of those five might provide the most helpful explanations.

Lastly, I will mention a group of scholars who have approached the concept of creativity in an entirely different way and regard it as something potentially negative. First, Chris Bilton has pointed to how creativity can have a dark side and potentially be a destructive concept because it can lead to an excessive focus on being innovative instead of creating value (Bilton 2015). In that piece, he plays with the idea of what uncreativity might be and the German sociologist Andreas Reckwitz has since made similar points (Reckwitz 2017). Another voice in this group is Jan Løhmann Stephensen who in publications and newspaper articles has warned people about the general obsession with creativity nowadays. His argument is that the idea that creativity can solve societal problems is misguided to some extent and that the general search for creativity can lead to a stressful life both at work and at home (Stephensen 2018). In my PhD dissertation, I too describe how the intention to maximize the creative input in, for example, idea development processes can put a lot of pressure on workers in media industries and how the intention to be radically creative might be more of an ideal and rarely the reality in organizations where smaller, incremental ideas often get accepted (Andersen 2019a). My argument for placing all of these works about the negative perspective on creativity in the social constructivist tradition is that they all regard creativity as a kind of construct and want to deconstruct it or debunk it.

I hope that this chapter's categorization and discussion of *the five traditions* has given you as readers a better idea of how creativity is a complex and multisided phenomenon. As mentioned in the beginning of the chapter, we can probably find even more ways to approach creativity. Therefore, if someone asks me how we can define creativity, I would say that there are *at least* five possible options. With the five traditions presented here, you have a useful tool for understanding creativity that also gives you five different ways of researching it, which the following chapters will describe in further detail. Although all models and tables are naturally reductive and oversimplify many complexities, I have summarized the insights from this chapter in the table below to make them even more tangible.

Table 2.1. Summary of the Five Traditions (Five Approaches to Creativity Research)

Tradition	Objectives	Advantages	Disadvantages
Individualist	To understand geniuses and intelligence, to find or measure creative personality traits	Can understand individuals and exceptionally gifted people	Creativity is not just reserved for individuals or geniuses
Sociocultural	To understand how social factors, cultural contexts and assessments also influence creativity	Can show how social ties, evaluations and motivations matter	Creativity is sometimes individual and not that social, low interest in the product itself
Pragmatic	To optimize products and control creative group processes through the use of tools and materials	Can actively manage creative group processes by e.g. introducing tools	Too focused on tools, products and corporate interests, low interest in people or individuals
Artistic	To assign authorship and criticize poor working conditions for workers	Can discuss political agendas and expose working conditions	Normative/political approach, low interest in creativity theory
Social Constructivist	To show how "creativity" and being "creative" is a social construction and potentially can be negative	Can show the negative sides of "creativity" and how people construct creative identities	May cause some degree of anti-essentialism or that you overlook the creation of something really original

Chapter 3

Media Industry Studies and Key Themes

This third chapter will present various contributions about media industries in order to connect them to creativity research and to relate the insights from chapter 2 to key themes concerning media industry studies. To make this connection more clear, the discussion will focus on three particular themes, which I see as fruitful intersections between both research fields. The first theme is *autonomy*, which will provide us with an understanding of how creative autonomy is a central part of the dynamics of work in media industries. The second theme is *nobody knows, which is an often-referenced theoretical concept about the unpredictability of cultural products and creative processes that this chapter will discuss and challenge. Lastly, the third and final theme in this chapter is idea development and gatekeeping*, which concerns theories about how ideas are developed, selected, and evaluated in the context of media industries.

This book focuses on the media industry side of media studies and on the production of media content because of my primary interest in the hidden and rarely studied creative processes that take place within these industries. This means that this particular book largely does not discuss audiences and consumers' impact on creativity or their understanding of the concept. While I indeed find that audience perspective interesting, it opens up quite different discussions and studies of users' creative actions on an everyday basis. In reality, we can describe these dynamics as cyclical and complex since consumer habits and audience reactions can affect media industries and their decisions about new creative products, which can again spark new trends among audiences. Subsequently, there is not enough room in this one book to cover such another vast perspective. By focusing only on media industries, it has been possible to create a more precise and pedagogical discussion of creativity, which is easier to navigate and understand for readers from media studies with no previous knowledge about creativity research.

In general, there are many connections between, on the one hand, the studies of *media industries* or media systems and, on the other hand, the studies of media production also known as *production studies* (Puijk 2016; Havens 2018). Historically, both fields have primarily focused on traditional or legacy media such as broadcasting media (radio and television), news media, and film. Because production studies is not only a research tradition but also an overall methodological approach, I will save the full discussion of production studies for the next chapter, which has a methodological focus.

For many years, studies of media industries and media production were caught in the middle of the disagreement between political economy (the Frankfurt school) and cultural studies (the Birmingham school) (Kellner 2009). While political economy scholars have frequently conducted structuralist studies of media production, cultural studies scholars have mostly conducted more interpretive and liberation-oriented studies of media production practices and practitioners. Yet, in recent years, we have gradually seen more and more examples that mix these two approaches, coming from North America, Europe (especially the UK), and Australia under the headline of "media industry studies" (e.g., Banks, Conor, and Mayer 2015; Dawson and Holmes 2012; Draper 2014; Havens and Lotz 2016; Holt and Perren 2009; Mayer, Banks, and Caldwell 2009). Another example of these new media industry studies would be the works published in the *Media Industries Journal* and in connection with their London conferences and in the media industry sections at other major media research associations' conferences. I would also situate this book within media industry studies and point to how the five traditions have presented perspectives from both cultural studies and political economy that you as readers can freely choose between or combine.

When it comes to media industries and creativity, very few media scholars have expressed an interest in discussing how these topics connect. As previously mentioned, Phillip McIntyre is one of these few with a media and humanities background who compares the creative conditions in several different areas of media production in his book *Creativity and Cultural Production—Issues for Media Practice* (2012). Therein he describes the particular conditions that apply to the production of different kinds of media like radio, television, journalism, film, photography, music, and digital media. His stance on creativity theory is quite clear since his book explicitly adopts Csikszentmihalyi's systems model but also references other contributions from creativity research. In comparison, my book seeks to represent many different tendencies in creativity research of equal importance through the framework of the five traditions. McIntyre's different chapters contain fruitful points about, for example, how journalists sometimes struggle with being creative every single day in very short-sighted processes and how a tight set of rules about style and format work well for some journalists but not for others (McIntyre 2012, 109). In relation to television production, McIntyre even mentions constraints (with reference to Negus and Pickering 2004) and explains how formatting and format bibles both enable and inhibit creative freedom in an industry with a constant demand for content to fill programming schedules (McIntyre 2012, 121). The last point is also true for streaming catalogs today. Yet, McIntyre occasionally uses anecdotal evidence when he relies on stories about how, for example, Shakespeare, Hemingway, or Lennon and McCartney worked (McIntyre 2012, 110–11), which is not an uncommon technique in creativity research but it really does not tell us much of general value about creativity in media industries. Apart from McIntyre and a few other media scholars (e.g., Kerrigan 2013), some of which I mention in chapter 2, it is fair to say that we need to work on finding and discussing the connections between creativity research and media industry studies, which the following sections will provide.

Autonomy in Media Industries

The issue of autonomy continues to be central in media industry studies. As the following section will show, the historically important influence from cultural studies still to this day affects how some media scholars approach autonomy as a concept. In this context, several contributions merit mentioning because they relate to how media institutions, their employees, and their production processes work while also restricting individuals' autonomy.

In his book *The Cultural Industries*, David Hesmondhalgh describes the overall ambivalence in these industries and the general changes that they have undergone since the 1980s: (1) The cultural industries have become global businesses; (2) Their ownership and organizational structures have changed radically; (3) The number of small- and medium-sized businesses has increased; (4) Digitalization has changed distribution, consumption, and production; (5) The transnational circulation of content has increased; (6) Audience research has become more important; (7) Government policies and regulations have altered and public ownership has been dismantled; (8) The amount of money spent on advertising has increased; (9) Subscriptions models are becoming more popular with, for example, streaming services; and (10) Promotion and advertising increasingly penetrates media "texts" of all kinds (Hesmondhalgh 2019, 5–6).

Hesmondhalgh's errand with this overview and his contributions in general is often to criticize the working conditions in the cultural (and media) industries, the ways in which companies restrict workers' autonomy and the apparent commercialization of these industries. As discussed earlier, this corresponds with the general outlook on creativity in the artistic tradition and it has close connections to the legacy from cultural studies where they choose to study cultural industries from the workers' point of view and critique why their autonomy should be restricted to serve capitalist purposes (Hesmondhalgh and Baker 2011). First, because he sees creative autonomy as a dialectic between creativity and commerce, it implicitly or unknowingly disregards the research contributions about constraints from, for example, psychology and design that have a pragmatic view on creative autonomy. Second, he does underline the overall ambivalence in the cultural industries—and we can indeed claim that there is a similar ambivalence regarding creative autonomy.

Another important and often-cited contribution about media industries and autonomy is John T. Caldwell's study of the American film and television industries, their production culture and self-reflexivity. Caldwell uses a more ethnographic approach or a cultural-industrial research method as he calls it in his book where he combines textual analyses of artifacts from the workplaces, interview with the workers, ethnographic observations, and economic/industry analyses (Caldwell 2008, 345). Regarding creativity, he describes the growing restrictions on authorship in that industry among other things and criticizes the formulaic use of so-called production bibles. He thereby implicitly assumes that greater autonomy for producers and workers in film and television would lead to greater creativity (Caldwell 2008, 197, 213). Yet, he never gives his definition of how he understands creativity. Just as with Hesmondhalgh's book, he points toward the lack of autonomy as a major problem without recognizing other traditions' (the pragmatic) perception of creativity and how constraints could actually be productive.

The degree of autonomy for individuals in the media industries is also a theme for Timothy Havens and Amanda D. Lotz in their book *Understanding Media Industries*. However, they explain the relationship between the individual and the organization by using three theoretical principles (Havens and Lotz 2016, 11). Their first principle is *circumscribed agency*, which describes how workers in the media industries have some degree of autonomy but always under a number of cultural and structural restrictions from the organization and its management. This mediation between structures and agents is of course not unique but similar to the ideas in both Csikszentmihalyi's work and Bourdieu's work as I discussed in chapter 2. Their second principle is *ideological uncertainty* where they point out that it is difficult for media organizations to predict the context in which users will receive their content. Finally, their third and last principle is about how media production takes place within particular *cultures of production*, which are isolated from audiences and where the embedded content producers reproduce particular quality- and genre-oriented conventions. At the same time, these principles can explain the existence of industry myths or *industry lore* as Havens and Lotz call them (Havens and Lotz 2016, 162). Industry lore comes from gut feelings or basic ideas about what the "best practice is" or notions about "what audiences like," which is why these myths are not necessarily true. By focusing on these concepts, Havens and Lotz try to give several explanations behind the ambivalence that exists around media production and the concept of autonomy in media industries where structural frameworks both limit and further employees' agency. Because of this, we can describe their approach as notably less normative compared to Hesmondhalgh's or Caldwell's concept of autonomy.

Instead of me choosing one side or the other in the general disagreement about autonomy between the artistic and pragmatic traditions in media and creativity research, I will merely point out that there are several options for us media scholars when it comes to the topic of creative autonomy. We can choose to see any particular constraint as a restriction on freedom *or* as both a limitation and a tool in a creative process. This is, however, not to say that we should ignore the importance of power structures in media industries and organizations. The later section about gatekeeping will discuss exactly such structures and how they relate to creative processes.

Nobody Knows—or the Need for Risk Reduction

The second theme is this chapter is the peculiar phrase "nobody knows," which I would like to discuss in detail. In his book *Creative Industries: Contracts between Art and Commerce* (2000), economist Richard E. Caves discusses the economic logics behind several different creative industries through, for example, patterns in their use of deals and contracts. Caves's approach is to use theory of contracts and economic organization where decision-making is rational and apply these principles to creative industries. Interestingly, he treats creative industries and their many "artists" as an entirely special area because he claims that creativity plays a bigger role here than in the rest of the economy (Caves 2000, 2).

Caves borrows the phrase *nobody knows* from William Goldman and uses film and television as examples of how executives in these industries, despite their use of pretesting and audience research, are unable to see into the future and predict the financial success or failure of a creative product at an early stage. Additionally, these kinds of creative productions include considerable and irretrievable *sunk costs* where you pay for the whole (and sometimes long) production process and you are unable to earn anything until much later—for example, in the production of films or computer games. In particular, he gives a couple of anecdotes about some failed Hollywood blockbuster film projects and describes them as *ten-ton turkeys* (which are of course unable to fly). He then points to how these films failed despite substantial studio investments, partly due to not enough budgetary control but also because of a misguided belief in the director's creative vision (Caves 2000, 136ff.). In his view, these circumstances make creative industries much riskier than traditional industrial endeavors such as microchip production. Caves's logical view of creative workers and most artistic educations for students is simply that the supply of these workers exceeds the demand in the creative industries. To him, all these conditions combined makes it a risky business to rely on the financial success of any products from creative industries.

Concerning the workforce in creative (or media) industries, it is true that the supply often exceeds the demand, which low salaries and relative unemployment rates compared to other industries can confirm. Many content areas within media are also characterized by a general trend toward the *intentional overproduction* of content (Havens and Lotz 2016, 32) since, for instance, the number of podcasts nowadays seems to greatly exceed the market's (or audience's) demand, also due to the fact that podcasts are relatively easy to produce. Therefore, if you only take an entirely rational and economic approach to these industries, to a career path as a creative worker or to an investment in podcasting, they all sound like financially ill-advised choices and this makes Caves's claims somewhat understandable.

However, I do not know any executives or managers in *any* areas of business who can flawlessly see into the future and predict all outcomes beforehand (even though that would be practical and financially attractive). Executives in creative industries do obviously have a need and a desire for *risk reduction*—but that is not the same as concluding that nobody knows anything. In my experience, an executive, editor, or manager in a media organization can know quite a lot about their specific content area and can often even identify where there is room for innovation. To be precise, a common issue is rather that their organizational structures encourage risk reduction and frequently reward small, incremental innovations rather than radical innovations in their development of new content (Andersen 2019b). With these conditions in mind, a more precise description would be "nobody dares" and to point to the structures that encourage risk reduction in particular media organizations. I would also argue that producers *can* gain valuable knowledge from pretesting and conducting audience research during both early and late stages of production—but of course, such efforts still do not provide any bulletproof guarantees for success (financial or otherwise). Advertising, social networks, press reactions, reviewers, opinion leaders or even influencers can play a significant role in how audiences perceive products and these complex dynamics can affect the fate of any kind of cultural content.

In fact, as demonstrated by Michael Pokorny and John Sedgwick, there is historical evidence that suggests that Hollywood films often do *not* fail financially but that they in general turn a profit (Pokorny and Sedgwick 2010), which might partially explain why the Hollywood film industry has dominated the global film market for decades (Olson 1999). In television, the question of whether the production company or the commissioning broadcaster runs the biggest risk, in fact, depends on which kind of financing model because of the difference between cost-plus or deficit financing (for further details, see Doyle 2013, 111–12). In comparison with other theories about media industries and creative production, Caves's characterization of creative industries focuses on these fixed and rather unfortunate economic conditions combined with high risks. If such a view prevails, it leaves little room for autonomy and even seems to advise creative industry organizations against taking any further risks. It is also difficult to find references to general creativity research in Caves's book apart from when he mentions gatekeepers and their motives as important in order to understand how creative industries work (Caves 2000, 21) with reference to Getzels and Csikszentmihalyi's study of art students (Getzels and Csikszentmihalyi 1976). Caves's approach somewhat echoes the pragmatic tradition from earlier because he compares creative industries to more efficient and reliable forms of industrial production. Furthermore, David Hesmondhalgh has criticized Caves for not addressing all the levels of inequality in these industries (Hesmondhalgh 2019, 100) even though Caves does describe the general financial conditions for creative industries as rather poor. To summarize, Caves's book is rather pragmatic and skeptical toward creative industries as a financial investment and, in terms of his approach to creativity, he provides no clear interest in or definition of the concept. Because of these downsides, I would recommend that we should not give his book (2000) much explanatory power in terms of understanding how creative processes in media industries actually work but regard it as an economist's evaluation of whether creative industries are profitable.

Finally, another aspect to consider is whether these industries themselves are interested in researching their own failures in depth or if they would rather keep quiet about them. The latter approach does of course make it easier for anyone in that industry to avoid making the same mistake in the future. If we encourage more studies of failed projects in media industries, we might be able to circumvent some of the above-mentioned issues and patterns.

Idea Development and Gatekeeping in Media Industries

In this section, I wish to discuss a number of contributions about idea development and gatekeeping in order to highlight how these exact aspects can make the abstract concept of creativity more tangible and usable in an analysis. Additionally, these two areas can be a fruitful intersection where several of the five traditions can contribute. That being said, there are of course many other subprocesses, which are relevant to look at using creativity theory.

When I mention idea development and gatekeeping under one headline, I wish to stress that these two areas are related and are important to consider when we study media industries.

Idea development is sometimes also called "ideation," "incubation," or "brainstorming" and we can trace the interest in this activity at least back to Alex Osborn's book *Applied Imagination* (1953) in which he introduces the technique behind brainstorming and creative problem-solving (Osborn 1953/1963). Most of the research I was able to find on idea development comes from psychology and design research. Since the goal of this book is not to become more creative but to research and understand creativity, I am rather uninterested in literature about how you can do brainstorming in practice and much more interested in analytical approaches to the evaluations of ideas and perceptions of creative processes.

How do we understand ideas? In everyday situations, we tend to talk about ideas as if they only have one owner. The importance of intellectual property (IP) and the threat of plagiarism permeate both (most) research communities and media industries and lead us to think about this kind of solitary ownership over particular ideas. However, when we develop ideas in practice it is common to collaborate by allowing a group to share an idea or by letting several people discuss the same idea at once (see Li, Shaw, and Olson 2013; Paulus and Nijstad 2003). Subsequently, we tend to talk about ideas as if they are fixed entities, while ideas in fact often change slightly or even drastically over time. Ideas sometimes even change after they become products, as is the case when we look at the computer games that are regularly updated, debugged, and maintained even years after their release. Research also suggests that we systematically value our own ideas and own works higher than others do (Buccafusco and Sprigman 2011), which means that we are perhaps generally too positive about our own ideas and unable to assess the actual value of our own creations accurately.

So what is an idea exactly? As Nanne Inie and Peter Dalsgaard have suggested in their literature review of idea development research, many of the general definitions of what an idea is are fairly vague. They illustrate how there are many different types of ideas ranging from ideas for very specific solutions to ideas that totally reinterpret the framing around the problem in question (Inie and Dalsgaard 2017). While they create a typology of ideas to show that there are many different kinds of ideas, I have chosen another approach in my own research.

I have previously studied how developers and editors evaluate ideas for television programming where I studied their development process using programming briefs, observations of developers, and interviews with editors as my empirical sources (Andersen 2019b). In that study, I chose to pay significant attention to idea development as a strategically important subprocess, which can be particularly crucial for people and departments in many media organizations and affect their ability to compete for audience attention. I also assume that idea development is a continuous process that many people have to do repeatedly as a part of their media work. This of course makes it more likely that they will get better at idea development but in my experience, it is also possible that they will grow slightly tired of the repeated need for new ideas. We might think of idea development as the very first and initial phase in media production, however, it is in reality a process that extends itself much further because media workers can add or revise aspects of the initial idea throughout both the production and post-production phase.

In this context, the major issue is that there are very few studies of actual idea development processes in media industries. In my search for such studies so far, I only managed to find a couple of contributions that are about actual idea development. One such article is by James Paul Roberts, who has written about idea development in television drama—but with a very specific focus on the imagined clash between creative and commercial agenda in that process. With this book's previous chapters in mind, it is perhaps not that surprising that his results show that creative and commercial agendas *can* coexist and that workers in the television industry can develop ideas using both these agendas without perceiving it as a problem (J. P. Roberts 2010). Additionally, Mats Nylund has looked at the idea development at editorial meetings in Finnish news production by using media management's approach to creativity. He describes how these Finnish journalists primarily get inspirations from other newspapers and have a difficult time developing ideas that are not already a part of the national news agenda (Nylund 2013). Such a finding supports the existence of domain-specific norms for idea development that relate to how specific professions such as journalists conduct their work. Here, it is equally relevant to mention Janet Fulton's work on journalism and creativity (e.g., Fulton 2011). Another study by Lars Harder and Rasmus Ladefoged describes how a programming concept (a short description of a new television show) in television production plays an important role in the development phase at a Danish production company. They explain how an editor can role play as the potential producer, client, or viewer in order to assess the viability of a new idea and how programming concepts communicate a not yet recorded "vision" (Harder and Ladefoged 2007, 130). What they do not describe, unfortunately, is how the actual idea development plays out or what happens during the pitching or idea selection sessions.

Still, I recognize some of the dynamics mentioned above from my own fieldwork and one particularly interesting moment is the *pitch*. While pitching ideas to either external clients or internal collaborators is a key aspect of work in many media industries, pitching has received very little academic attention from media scholars and is mostly frequently mentioned in the how-to-do-advertising literature. During my fieldwork and during educational collaborations with media companies, I have observed several pitching sessions. Much like the programming concepts, many pitches are only specific about selected aspects of the suggested product and this creates room for the client's own interpretation to affect what the not yet actualized idea "could be." In reality, the idea can change even during a short pitching session due to the client's wishes, and because of this the people that pitch usually need to bring a flexible idea (Andersen 2019a). Not surprising, the reason is that some clients or editors like to feel agency, to be able to put their own impression on the idea, or to fill in the blanks.

Another key aspect in idea development is the *brief*. A brief is a short, written summary that outlines what the idea development should deliver. Some idea development processes might not use briefs altogether or perhaps rely solely on verbal briefing about the requirements—for instance, for journalists who sometimes need to do idea development on a daily basis. Ana Alačovska has written about the use of briefs for travel guidebook writers who are often freelancers. She describes how a very detailed editorial brief functions as a management tool, which gives them a strong control over travelling freelance writers and helps to ensure that the editors receive a consistent and reliable product that fits the market needs and the appropriate target group (Alačovska 2013, 173). Interestingly, one of her guidebook writers called Daisy expresses great satisfaction with getting a very detailed brief with lots of constraints from her publisher because she feels it improves her texts and it gives her comfort to know exactly what she needs to deliver in order to get recognition and possibly a new contract afterward (Alačovska 2013, 175). Although Alačovska seems to be using the romantic everyday definition of creativity, Daisy's perspective on detailed briefs fits well with the insights from the pragmatic tradition that discuss constraints as also being a resource.

In that case and in many other cases, the role of the editor is to be a gatekeeper that developers face during a creative process. The term *gatekeeper* is mostly used in journalism research and ascribed to Kurt Lewin (1943) who defined a gatekeeper as an individual or group in a decisive position with the right to decide if something or someone is allowed to proceed or is rejected. In journalism research, gatekeeping commonly refers to how editors select news stories and articles both at an individual and organizational level (Shoemaker 1991; Shoemaker and Vos 2009). In David Manning White's classic study of a telegram editor at a small Midwestern morning paper who he calls "Mr. Gates," he states how this gatekeeper has selected which news stories to print based on highly subjective evaluation criteria and personal taste (White 1950). Here I am reminded of an albeit old but still relevant story from Guilford about how teachers (or in White's case, editors and managers) often are more likely to support the ideas that are similar to their own (Guilford 1950, 448).

Contributions from cultural production have discussed the same distribution of roles but in a slightly different way. Keith Negus has written about cultural industries and music where the gatekeeper (e.g., a producer) sometimes prefers to actively seek out potential talents and help reshape their products at an early stage before they are finished (Negus 2002, 510). He mentions editors, talent scouts, and producers as gatekeepers in music production, which are roles that we can also find in many media industries. If we think of, for example, television, other gatekeepers can be audiences, buyers and distributors who sell content on national or international markets (e.g., Jensen 2018, DiMaggio and Hirsch 1976, 739) or even cultural intermediaries such as reviewers, cultural journalists, media "personalities," and other new kinds of amateur reviewers, micro celebrities, or influencers (e.g., Bourdieu 1984; From and Kristensen 2014).

One particularly relevant case study in this context comes from Jimmy Draper who has studied the relationship between writers and editors at three American men's magazines. Even though Draper seems to have been looking for issues around interpretations of masculinity, he also delivers interesting findings about the dynamics of gatekeeping. Draper uses the term *discerned savvy* to refer to the knowledge that employees in media industries have about their superiors' preferences and tastes, which they can then use to shape their ideas during idea development (Draper 2014, 1126). Despite these taste hierarchies, his informants still express how they feel a great degree of creative autonomy and freedom even though they have just disclosed how they purposefully only select the ideas that fit their editor's taste. Draper also refers to Havens and Lotz's concept of circumscribed agency (Havens and Lotz 2016, 161ff.), however, his concept of discerned savvy describes a very particular dynamic that I recognize from studying and working with media organizations. I suggest that discerned savvy even applies to group dynamics where developers in a group sometimes help each other by sharing knowledge about gatekeeping editors' tastes. In my particular case study of television, their group-validation turned out to be a valuable tool and they knew rather precisely when they came up with a particular idea that it was a perfect fit for their boss's taste. Eventually, they were right and their boss approved that particular idea instantly (Andersen 2019b) and this shows how discerned savvy might very well be a key feature of creative processes in some media industries.

As a final addition to this section about the gatekeeping of ideas in media industries, I will include Keith Sawyer's work on evaluative regimes. Even though it is not strictly about media industries and gatekeepers, I will argue that it has close ties to the discussion of such dynamics. In line with the sociocultural and social constructivist traditions, a normative evaluation decides whether something is creative or not within a specialized field, which contains established norms and practices. Sawyer's contribution here supports that perspective as he argues that it is vital to study evaluation practices because creative processes often are collective and involve creators and various gatekeepers evaluating and assessing products. Just like in educational research, Sawyer distinguishes between formative evaluation, where the evaluation takes place during the creation process, and summative evaluation, which is the final evaluation after the process ended. Sawyer's chapter looks at all the other business cases in the same book (Moeran and Christensen 2013) and points out how most evaluations fall into four categories or so-called evaluative regimes where they assess and value products based on specific and subjective criteria (Sawyer 2013, 281):

1. An *aesthetic* regime based on whether the product design is new and interesting
2. A *craft/professional* regime based on whether the product is well made and lives up to a professional standard
3. A *manufacturing* regime based on whether the product can be made in a reliable way and at a reasonable cost
4. A *brand/genre* regime based on whether the product fits the brand in question and meets the genre expectations

In his construction of these categories, Sawyer draws on Georg Simmel's claim that value is not inherent to objects but socially and subjectively defined (Simmel 1978) and on Arjun Appadurai's work, which uses four distinctions similar to Sawyer's (Appadurai 1986). According to Sawyer, professionals in creative industries may use several of his regimes at once and they are often rather strategic about how they phrase their evaluations especially when the developer or the client is present in the room (Sawyer 2013, 286, 289). Furthermore, he underlines the importance of reputation for both companies and individuals, which plays into the evaluations that their products receive. Like Draper, he explains how developers already before the presentation or pitch anticipate how gatekeepers might evaluate the product and that a key motivational factor is to create and sell a product that gives you a good reputation or looks nice on your CV (Sawyer 2013, 296). However, Sawyer warns both other researchers and industry professionals about putting too much emphasis on success stories without studying the failed products and rejected ideas.

Although Sawyer's four categories are quite generic so that they can fit the different creative processes in various industries, I have found them to be rather useful as an analytical tool (Andersen 2019b) that helps the researcher within exposing some of the discursive and social mechanisms in evaluative processes. I can only stress that this particular theoretical area around autonomy, idea development, and gatekeeping, in my opinion, has a lot of potential for media research where there is still much left for us to study.

This chapter has introduced many relevant contributions about autonomy, nobody knows, idea development, and gatekeeping. However, despite these contributions, it is fair to say that there are still many gaps and blank spaces in the existing research about these exact topics. I believe that creativity theory can provide us with some of the essential tools to fill in the blanks, which I will discuss in detail in the last chapter. In the following chapter, I will present how media production studies is a valuable methodological approach for our studies of creativity.

Chapter 4

Production Studies as a Methodological Approach

This chapter discusses what we can call the first tier of methodology and what it means to use production studies as our overall approach. It will explain how you can do a production study in media industries, why this approach can be particularly rewarding and how you can combine different methods within it. Conducting a production study can also create certain practical challenges because you ultimately need to get access to the people working in the media industries, which can influence your study in various significant ways. The four key themes in this chapter will be *production studies in general*, *access*, *data collection,* and *the importance of time* as well as how it affects your production study.

Production Studies in General

This book suggests media production studies or production analysis as the overall methodological approach for studies of creativity in media industries. Media production studies are sociological studies of the "senders" behind media content. The goal in such studies is to shed a light on these production and creation processes in media that are often hidden and invisible to the public. The medium in question can be all kinds of media and the methods used for production studies are often interviews and participant observations but sometimes even policy analysis, historical analysis, or document analysis (Karppinen and Moe 2011; Van den Bulck et al. 2019; Redvall and Bruun 2022). The methodological advantage behind conducting a media production study is that it can provide us with new information about the organizational processes. A classic example in this case would be Hortense Powdermaker's ethnographic study of the American film industry (Powdermaker 1950).

Historically speaking, production studies come from a mixture of many different scientific traditions such as media sociology, organizational studies, auteur studies, political economy, cultural studies, ethnography, journalism, and critical theory (Havens 2018). There is also a strong tradition of what they call "newsroom studies" in journalism research where they, since the 1950s, have done many ethnographical studies of the conditions and work patterns of news journalists (e.g., Cottle 2007; Gans 1980; Hassall Thomsen 2013; Paterson and Domingo 2008; Schlesinger 1979; Willig 2011; White 1950). Production studies and newsroom studies often study relatively familiar environments (sometimes similar to the researcher's own background in both language and culture) and are typically not studies of foreign and exotic cultures even though they borrow methods such as participant observation from ethnography. In comparison to media industry studies, those research efforts tend to look at broader, macro-oriented tendencies in the media landscape, while production studies have a micro-oriented interest in the smaller details of specific media productions. We can also argue that production studies share many similarities with organizational analysis (see DiMaggio and Hirsch 1976) except that production studies of course focus more on production processes whereas organizational analysis tends to have an interest in other themes such as management and leadership. Here we must also consider at what level of the organization we wish to conduct our study since media organizations (especially the larger, hierarchical ones) have several levels ranging from the management/strategic level to the production team level comprised of more ordinary workers (Newcomb and Lotz 2002).

Throughout the last half of the 20th century, media scholars conducted some of the first and crucial media production studies of, for instance, television production (e.g., Alvarado and Buscombe 1978; Gitlin 1983; Gripsrud 1995; Newcomb and Alley 1983). However, during the latest 10–15 years, there has been a visible increase in the amount of publications concerning media production studies. All of these new works play a key part in establishing this field as an important area of research for both media researchers and media industry professionals (e.g., Bakøy, Puijk, and Spicer 2017; Banks, Conor, and Mayer 2015; Batty et al. 2019; Caldwell 2008; Hammett-Jamart, Mitric, and Novrup Redvall 2019; Mayer, Banks, and Caldwell 2009; Mayer 2013; Ozimek 2018; Redvall 2014; Szczepanik and Vonderau 2013; Sotamaa and Švelch 2021; Sundet 2021b; van Keulen 2021). Despite these many new contributions, however, only a fraction of them contain explicit discussions of the many methodological challenges and issues that you can experience when you conduct production studies. In this context, it is mostly these contributions that are particularly relevant to the methodological discussion (Batty and Kerrigan 2018; Bruun 2014; Bruun and Frandsen 2017, Frandsen 2007; Mayer 2008; Paterson et al. 2016; Puijk 2008; Redvall and Bruun 2022; Sundet 2021a; Ytreberg 2000).

Within the sociologically and organizationally oriented production studies, we often find two classic issues. The first issue concerns the old disagreements between political economy and cultural studies about whether we should give the credit and explanatory power behind cultural productions to systemic and structural powers or to individuals' actions and interpretations (Frandsen 2007; Bruun 2011). The second issue concerns how production studies can focus primarily on texts and actors or on contexts and structures but often struggle to explain the links *between* these two elements (Ytreberg 2000). It is not that easy to describe in accurate terms how structures affect people and vice versa in a particular media production when you actually get to experience the intricate dynamics inside a production process. As Espen Ytreberg points out, production studies can contribute by *studying how media professionals' discursive interpretations and mutual negotiations of previous productions affect their text production* (Ytreberg 2000). For myself, this point has been particularly eye opening as it makes you think about what it is like to work on a media production and how your experiences with previous productions contribute to the social negotiations of what "good" and "bad" production practices are. This means that the *value* of a previously produced text is not necessarily given or fixed but can change over time—as I also realized was true for the case in one of my previous production studies (Andersen 2017). In this way, Ytreberg sees text production and text interpretation as mutually constituting (Ytreberg 2000, 54–55). With this in mind, it makes good sense to study how industry professionals themselves perceive and experience the media industrial conditions under which they work and how their self-reflexivity and interpretations of previous productions affect their work (Caldwell 2008). Such an approach makes the people inside the productions crucial sources of information if we are to understand the actions and motivations of particular media organizations.

Lastly, we can distinguish between working *forwards* or *backwards* in production studies. When doing a production study forwards, we are studying a particular production in situ as it is happening. While this sounds like the ideal way to gain sociological insights about the production, the reality is that it can both be difficult to get the access and timing in place. As a result, we can sometimes only do the production study backwards, which means that we can draw on retrospective data and sources that contain a valuable knowledge about a particular production's history, events, and details. While such backwards studies are still valid contributions, they can contain ambivalence or even oversimplified explanations that are difficult to challenge for the researcher who needs to ensure the validity of the study (Bruun and Frandsen 2017, 124). Finally, another option can also be to combine forwards and backwards production studies—especially if you are trying to study, for instance, the development of a particular genre over time. This is what Ytreberg calls *the exchange strategy* where we as researchers invest a considerable amount of time by collecting data over a long period in order to document and analyze developments in the production of texts and genres over time (Ytreberg 2000, 56–57).

Access

After the more general considerations about production studies, this section will discuss the specific and important challenge of getting *access* to people and productions.

A production study ultimately requires access. This means that we must contact the relevant people in a particular media industry and organization(s) and kindly ask them to let us talk to them and possibly visit their workplace. An obvious option is for you to negotiate access in a formal way with them and sign a mutual agreement, contract or non-disclosure agreement (NDA). Alternatively, you can approach them in a more informal way by just negotiating a verbal agreement about the conditions of your access as a researcher. However, some organizations seem to reject all access requests from researchers. As Vilde Schanke Sundet has pointed out recently, major streaming companies or global media platforms (such as Google, YouTube and Netflix), which many researchers would like to get in touch with, are notoriously closed off (Sundet 2021a). Because of this need for access, a production study always comes with the risk of not getting access or losing the access at some point (if they decide to take it away from you). This loss of control can feel scary for some researchers who are used to being the sole managers of their studies. Until you have some kind of agreement with the media organization in question, you cannot know if the study is feasible or if you can get access to a specific subprocess or part of their production.

When we approach industry professionals and ask for access, it can sometimes be effective to appear friendly, give them praise and target your communication toward the specific organization, department, and person that you wish to persuade (Bruun 2014). As some of my previous students found out, sending out the same template-email to a bunch of different organizations and people at once can be rather ineffective. Of course, it also helps to have a large network of personal contacts, to have a friend of a friend inside the organization who can vouch for you, or to have work experience within that industry or specific organization (the latter situation helped in studies such as Dornfeld 1998; Grindstaff 2002). In my experience, many industry professionals are happy that an academic is finally taking an interest in their production practice and this can be an advantage in access negotiations.

In terms of ethics, you need to live up to the principle of informed consent (Kvale and Brinkmann 2015, 116ff.) and make sure that they know what your errand in their organization is. However, in my own experience, they can also be skeptical of your choice of focus or simply worried that you are doing undercover work, going to reveal their corporate secrets or going to write news articles about them (see also Puijk 2008, 33). It can require significant diplomatic skills to assure them that this is not your mission. I have been in situations with paranoid informants who were skeptical of my presence in their organization and it was difficult for me to convince them that I was not going to betray their confidence. Even though some words can be triggering (so try to use a somewhat harmless language), I still to this day have no idea what I did to trigger that reaction on their part and I cannot explain why some organizational members become paranoid. I can only confirm that it is a challenge that you need to be aware of when you conduct your access negotiations.

Once these negotiations are over, you know what kind of access you have and that largely dictates what your study can do (Frandsen 2007, 44ff.). Here, Kirsten Frandsen distinguishes between access *as a gift* and access *as a trade*. In the first instance, we get access freely without giving anything back to the organization. While that sounds alluring, it can unfortunately make the researcher feel a debt to the organization and make it difficult to conduct a critical study of their practices because they can quickly remove your access again if they dislike your criticisms. In the second instance, you give something back to the organization, which can be a report, a presentation, a quantitative analysis or some other kind of work effort that benefits them. The advantage of this access as a trade is that the power dynamic becomes more equal since both sides get something out of the cooperation (Frandsen 2007, 48–49).

Data Collection

Once you have your access in place, you need to navigate inside the organization, to choose what you wish to focus on based on the available possibilities and to start collecting data. You can use various qualitative or quantitative methods, as we will discuss in the next section.

When you do a production study, it is in my opinion important to *keep your analytical distance*. By that, I mean that I want to give myself the possibility to be critical of their work if I need to be. It also means that you should be skeptical toward undocumented industry lore or trade stories (Caldwell 2008). When I supervise students, I at times also refer to *the sales pitch* that some industry informants seem to be keen on giving you where they primarily focus on their most successful productions and on only the positive aspects of their work. While the sales pitch may not be the most reliable single source of information, it can still be useful to your study. If you have a data source that documents their actual production practices, you can compare it with the sales pitch and use that comparison to highlight potential inconsistencies and self-contradictions in their narrative about their work.

A common pitfall in production studies is *overexplaining*. Because production practices are hidden and invisible to the public, the researcher can easily become much too preoccupied with explaining all of the intricate details of how production happens and which roles and actions all the different production members carry out. As a result, some production studies focus almost exclusively on gathering empirical data (Bruun and Frandsen 2017, 120) and on telling the production's story. This tendency toward the descriptive is understandable since detailed media production studies can be few and rare in particular countries. While the large empirical material and the many long explanations of production practices can still be relevant, the cost is that these studies tend to have less of an interest in applying theories, discussing methods, or presenting actual analytical results. My recommendation in this area going forward is that instead of telling production *stories*, we should focus on doing production *studies*, which live up to all of the necessary academic requirements instead of being purely descriptive.

The Importance of Time

During your production study and your data collection, *time* is a very important parameter. You cannot always control the time and timing that can dictate your options inside the organization(s) that you study (Bruun and Frandsen 2017; Ryfe 2016). In addition, no matter which media industry you are studying, that particular medium's production logics can create particular constraints for your study. Media productions can often have long and continuous processes of production and development. This is especially true for the long and/or slow forms of media production such as gaming, film, and certain television genres. If you are instead studying the short and/or fast media industries such as news journalism or podcasting, the challenge is often that you may need to adapt to their quick processes and, for instance, spend more time in a short period if you wish to document a singular production before they move on to the next. Particular media genres can also contain specific conditions which you may need to adapt to and here there is a difference between fiction and factual productions (Bruun and Frandsen 2017, 122). For instance, in the production of documentaries, factual television and different kinds of journalism, you may have to act very quickly in order to study the process. However, feature films and television fiction can have longer processes of scriptwriting where you as a researcher have many opportunities to visit them during that process (Redvall 2014; Conor 2010; Pjajčíková and Szczepanik 2015). Depending on the writers' tempo, it could take years if you want to document the whole writing process from start to finish. Documenting a whole media production from the idea development to the launch or premiere can also prove to be an extremely time-consuming task. Overall, this means that we can help ourselves by finding and formulating specific analytical focus points in our production study to avoid spending too much time or gathering too much data.

This chapter has discussed many different aspects of production studies as a methodological approach, which is valuable to us as researchers as long as we reflect on the challenges involved. This chapter has focused exclusively on production studies but not on how having creativity as your topic creates methodological challenges. Therefore, in the next chapter, I will reflect on the many kinds of challenges that almost inevitably will arise when we set out to research the topic of "creativity" in media industries.

Chapter 5

Challenges When Researching Creativity

The two most recent chapters have set the scene for this fifth chapter by defining how we can understand media industries (chapter 3) and how we can use production studies as an approach (chapter 4). With these two elements in place, we are now ready to proceed to reflect on *how creativity as a research focus creates methodological challenges* when doing production studies of media industries. Since the few existing works about creativity in media industries do not thoroughly discuss the methodological challenges that occur in such studies, I consider the following considerations to be one of this book's most important contributions to the field of media studies.

The chapter here contains three sections with specific methodological themes. The first section is about *where* creativity is and where it probably is not. In this context, we will also discuss how we can handle the challenge of normativity. The second section is about how to *document* creativity when it is so notoriously elusive and discusses the challenges of working with *qualitative and quantitative methods* to research creativity. Finally, the third section is about how we can be mindful of *industry-specific logics and genre perceptions*.

Where is Creativity?

If you have been paying attention, this book should have made it clear by now that there is serious doubt about whether creativity can be "found" at all. The question in this section's headline was originally posed by Csikszentmihalyi (1988) as a way of reorienting the discussion from "what" to "where" is creativity. As a reminder, he does in fact believe that we can find creativity. If you are planning a study of creativity and you have not yet made up your mind about whether creativity exists out in the world or not, you need to reflect on how *you* understand it, and which of the five traditions you find most appropriate. However, if we for a while set aside the social constructivist tradition, in which we cannot really find creativity as such, we can focus on how we might otherwise find it and study it.

In general, the whole issue around finding creativity actually depends on how you choose your *case within the case* (Thomas 2015). I often distinguish between the overall top-level case(s), which is usually the organization(s), and the case within the case that contains the selected people, roles, and processes that I specifically analyze. Depending on the nature of the case study and your research question, the findings from your case study can be of a unique and intrinsic nature or of a more general and instrumental nature (Stake 2005).

We could utter the sweeping statement that creativity is everywhere. At least, as I have described in chapter 2, some researchers operate with the belief that creativity is in all everyday actions. While that is a nice thought and allows you to study anything, it really does not help you with identifying a course of action. My best advice regarding where to find creativity is that it is important to delimit your object of study. Narrow it down. One group of people, one professional role or one subprocess might be plenty for you (depending on your research question) and easier than trying to describe and analyze all creative processes inside a whole organization. I have seen students working with creativity who easily lose their way inside an organization because they are trying to analyze all the actions and processes as some kind of creativity. If you instead give yourself *a stopping point*, you prevent yourself from going on for too long. That stopping point can be a point in time when a certain stage of a process is over or when you are only finding repetitions of already uncovered findings.

Another challenge that I mentioned in chapter 3 is the issue around who "owns" ideas and products—especially while they are still being developed. Here I am not referring to issues around copyright or IP but to issues of creative ownership in a more abstract or emotional way. Unless you are studying an individual in an industry or several people working very individually (e.g., a book author working alone), you are most likely studying someone who collaborates with many others and is a part of a team of some kind. Who then "has" the creativity? Well, when you study a group of media professionals, remember the previous collectivist insights about how several people can take ownership over the same idea at once and use it at the same time. Be mindful of the condition that the content and value of an idea or product can change over time and sometimes without others noticing it. In practice, this means that you should keep your eyes open and look out for the sociocultural group dynamics if you are trying to study, for example, a group's idea development session or a pitch meeting.

On the flip side, where is creativity probably not? Again, the mindset and the preconceptions that you have about creativity will probably lead you down specific paths. If your background is in authorship studies and you are studying, for example, film production, you are probably looking for a best practice, for particular moments of glory, or for how you can attribute credit to particularly skilled or visionary members of the production team. Here the question of "where is creativity not?" can be useful to stimulate reflections about what you are perhaps overlooking, such as the work of people in less artistic roles. For instance, it surprises me how little research there is about casters and the casting processes in media industries. Even though casting as a preproduction process has a major impact on the subsequent production— and is common in both film, television, video games, commercials, and so forth— we do not know much about the intricate details and dynamics of casting in all these media industries. Additionally, the strong focus on content production as creative in media industries research might lead to fewer studies about distributors and aggregators of various kinds. In Havens and Lotz's book about media industries, they exactly have this somewhat strange distinction between "creative practices" and "distribution and aggregation practices" (Havens and Lotz 2016, 27). Although it is understandable that they think differently about content production compared to content aggregation or distribution, we can definitely challenge their distinction since aggregating and distributing content can just as well require curation strategies and creative problem-solving. As chapter 6 will discuss, we can design studies that focus narrowly on a particular process but while being receptive to unexpected influences that turn out to play a crucial part in the creative process.

Another big methodological challenge is *normativity*. When we research creativity, we can very easily end up making normative judgment calls about what is creative and what is not. If you are comfortable with being normative in your work, then you might not think of this as an issue. If you, like me, are striving for impartiality as an ideal in your research efforts, normativity can become a challenge. I have experienced on a few occasions that other researchers have read my work as normative and interpreted it as if I had written positively about an organization or production that I merely wanted to analyze. This probably happened because I used the word creative and because the readers were interpreting it using the positive everyday definition of creativity. Due to this risk of being misunderstood, I try to stress the fact that I am not making judgment calls but simply trying to analyze creative practices while keeping an objective outlook on the case. My typical advice to both students and colleagues writing about creativity is that you should try to include both positive and negative aspects about your case in the analysis to avoid these misunderstandings.

How Can We Document Creativity?

When we have chosen one group of people, one professional role, or one subprocess to focus on, it is time to plan how we can document creativity.

Due to the many mysteries surrounding creativity, there is a real danger of over-documenting it. In order to compensate for the concept's relativity, the researcher or student typically tries to exaggerate the empirical documentation. The unfortunate result can be what Kvale and Brinkmann have called the *1000-page question* (Kvale and Brinkmann 2015, 166ff.), where the researcher becomes paralyzed by an overwhelming amount of empirical documentation. If you are using creativity as an analytical concept for the first time, be aware of this danger. In my own experience, the 1000-page question can also occur when you conduct an exploratory study without having any idea about what aspects about creativity you want to find and document.

In terms of documentation in general, you should look at your research question and ask yourself if it calls for qualitative or quantitative answers or both. The following sections will discuss these methodological choices.

Interviewing About Creativity

If you choose to use qualitative methods—such as interviews, participant observations, focus groups, diaries, and so forth— to research creativity, you have to strategize about how you will document it while still avoiding the 1,000-page question.

One way of circumventing that problem is to focus on how your informants understand creativity and act based on their understanding of it. By asking them about what we, with a new concept, can call their degree of *creative awareness*, you avoid having to prove creativity in itself because it allows you to highlight your informants' reflections and language about creativity. They often express this awareness as self-reflexivity about their actions at work where we can learn how they see their own life-world and what being creative means to them. How can we then get them to express their creative awareness? In interviews, I have sometimes found it useful to ask an open question such as "Can you explain what you do in a typical workday" or "What is a good idea" (or bad idea) based on their own work experience. This approach was inspired by Stephanie Taylor's work as mentioned earlier and by the use of self-reflexivity as a rather common theme in production studies due to John T. Caldwell's use of the concept (Caldwell 2008). It simply tells us quite a lot when we get interviewees to talk about their professional role or about a particularly good or bad product. What kind of language or discourse do they use to describe it? What aspect of the product or the production process do they highlight when they evaluate it? Just like Keith Sawyer has used these evaluative regimes (Sawyer 2013) to study assessments of creative products, we can document the language and the awareness of creativity that informants express. If the informant in question is some kind of gatekeeper, their evaluations of creativity are particularly valuable and important to examine closely. Generally, we can often describe interviewees in the media industries as so-called *exclusive informants* who possess a crucial knowledge about some specific process in their organization (Bruun 2014). These informants are exclusive when they are difficult to replace with someone else and they sometimes have privileged and powerful positions within that particular industry. Even though many creation processes in media production are collective, informants may still be closely guarded and manage the access to the knowledge about their production in a careful way.

Additionally, informants can easily have several different definitions of creativity in play at once without noticing it themselves (Taylor 2013) and it is common that they even contradict themselves or seem ambivalent (Kvale and Brinkmann 2015, 52) when they talk about creative work. I have also experienced informants that have declared openly that they want to be more creative but do not understand how creativity works and that they have given up on controlling it at all. Therefore, even though informants may have a creative awareness or a desire to optimize their creativity, they may not have the tools to do so. In summary, it can be useful to take an interest in your informants' creative awareness when you use interviews as a research method.

Observing Creativity

If you use participant observation as a method and wish to observe workers in a particular media industry, it is customary in anthropology and ethnography to write so-called *thick descriptions* or diaries about your observations (Geertz 1975). These are written representations of the culture(s) you observe, which can also be online if you do digital ethnography or "netnography" (Kozinets 2012; Pink 2016). When you plan and conduct these observations, you need to decide how much you are going to participate in the events you wish to document. If your degree of participation is low, you try to influence the unfolding events as little as possible (Hammersley and Atkinson 1995, 104). If your degree of participation is high, you embrace your own intervention into the unfolding events and acknowledge that the researcher's presence affects the surrounding social dynamics. I usually prefer to stay rather passive and silent while I hope that the workers will forget that I am present in the room and act as they would normally. Sometimes they do but they usually do seem to be aware of the researcher's presence and probably adjust parts of their behavior due to this.

During observational fieldwork, how do you then "follow" creativity? Herein lies a challenge because research shows that it is difficult to predict, for example, when and where inspiration hits people and they get a new idea (Coughlan and Johnson 2008). If you study someone's idea development process and you do not follow them around the clock, it is possible that you will be absent when (or if) they experience a significant inspiration or realization. I naïvely thought that my informants would get their ideas during the planned idea development sessions on the workdays that I observed. In reality, they came up with ideas in unpredictable, irregular rhythms and at moments in time when I was not paying attention. Because of this, my observations mostly consisted of watching them struggle with idea development during the planned idea development sessions. However, instead of trying to follow them everywhere at all times, I chose to focus on what I could learn about them in these struggling moments and on identifying that, which was perhaps holding them back.

Another important aspect in these kind of qualitative studies is to distinguish between first-order and second-order concepts. John Van Maanen has described *first-order concepts* as the empirical words used by the informants while the *second-order concepts* are the theoretical concepts that the researcher uses to explain the events (Van Maanen 1979). In one of my own studies of creativity, the actual word "creativity" was primarily a second-order concept used by me. The media workers in my study instead used the word "experimenting" or talked in broader terms about "ideas." However, over time I realized that we meant the same thing even though we used different words and that despite their use of the word *experiment*, they actually struggled very much with living up to their own expectations for how creative they wanted these so-called experiments to be (Andersen 2019a).

I found that working with observations can be quite challenging and I think it has to do with the narrative nature of participant observation as a method. Documenting one's personal experiences during that kind of fieldwork always depends on the narrative that the researcher uses to describe the events since no one can go out afterward and verify it or repeat the exact same process, which creates this rather inescapable dilemma for observational studies (Van Maanen 1979, 549). Doing this kind of fieldwork is an inherently subjective experience, which to me is very different from doing an interview, which I can document with a recording and a transcription. Concerning my field notes and observations during my PhD study, I did not know how to manage these sources and it took me many months to figure out how to include them. The reason was that I had to construct a fitting narrative about my experiences and at the same time accept my own subjective role as an ethnographer or observer. However, the strength in observations is exactly the ability to communicate these subjective experiences and phenomenological explanations.

Since observations like these can be rather one-sided, it can be a very good idea to combine them with other methods that can validate your claims (Bruhn Jensen 2002, 242–43).

Researching Creativity with Quantitative Methods

If you instead choose to work with quantitative methods—such as content analysis, surveys, databases, and so forth— then you have to make up your mind about whether or not you believe that you can quantify and measure creativity in itself. As I mentioned in chapter 2, there are researchers, especially in the individualist tradition, that still to this day believe that we can measure someone's creativity and give it a score (and if you agree, seek out their works). In my own work, I have so far focused on using quantitative methods to give an overview of what we can call the *creative output* or the patterns and amounts of content production within a particular media industry or organization and we can of course use quantitative methods to study many different useful aspects. In particular, such an overview of their creative output can be very helpful in the beginning of a case study of creativity to establish *what* and *how much* the organization does, which is valuable quantitative knowledge about them for you as a researcher. You can then use that knowledge in at least two ways: First, you can use your quantitative knowledge to identify specific areas of interest that you wish, for example, to ask your informants about in subsequent interviews. Second, you can try to use your quantitative knowledge in access negotiations with that organization about giving you access (as a trade—as mentioned in chapter 4) in exchange for you sharing your quantitative knowledge with them about their creative output.

To students, I generally recommend combining qualitative and quantitative methods (also called mixed methods). If we wish to understand a complex, multifactor phenomenon like creativity in media industries, I believe that it is important that we research it from many different angles and by using various methods. Additionally, if we want to research creativity in a large media organization, it can even make good sense to do multisited research (Falzon 2009; Marcus 1995) and study several different sites (places, people, processes, etc.) within that same organization.

Industry-Specific Logics and Genre Perceptions

In general, we can point to how there is an overall media logic that influences our society and makes us adapt to what works well "in the media" (e.g., Altheide and Snow 1979; Hjarvard 2016; Thimm, Anastasiadis, and Einspänner-Pflock 2018; McIntyre 2012). Underneath all of that, in any particular media industry, we can find *industry-specific logics and genre perceptions* in a configuration that is rather special for that one kind of media. For example, the radio industry has a certain set of naturalized logics, ways of thinking, and ways of doing radio. Because radio as a medium has a long history, it has well-established genres and has many radio professionals who have experience with how different production conditions affect the creation of radio content. If we then did a study of creativity in radio without knowing that industry beforehand, we would soon find that radio professionals to some extent share some common industry-specific logics, genre perceptions, and opinions about production. These industry-specific conventions can mostly be challenging for us as researchers if we are unaware of them and overlook how they influence creative processes. In a study of creativity in that industry, it might even be particularly valuable to make exactly these naturalized industry-specific logics visible in order to assess them as constraints and discuss if someone should challenge them. Another example here is Trine Syvertsen's work on the industry logics in television production in the 1990s (Syvertsen 1997), which can still explain much about how the television industry works today (at least in the Nordic countries) and proves that these industry-specific logics can be rather stable even despite the technological advancements that have affected the television medium.

Furthermore, all media industries use *genres* in their work to some extent. Havens and Lotz discuss such conventions within particular genres and cultures of production and highlight how they can "restrict" both aesthetic and ideological creativity. However, they also state that "[g]enres help guarantee that new media content will find an appropriate and willing audience and make the job of marketing easier because the new media good can be situated among previous goods" (Havens and Lotz 2016, 14). Therefore, while they describe genres as conventions that restrict, it is clear from the quote that genres are also constraints that just as well *enable* new products to receive positive feedback for being for instance creative within that genre (see also McIntyre 2012, 125ff.). If a new media product receives praise for mixing genres in an innovative way, we could argue that the conventionality in those preexisting genres simultaneously enabled that someone could label the new product as creative.

Another example of the effects of genre perceptions comes from my studies of people in the television industry and concerns how they perceive reality television as a genre. Due to the bad societal reputation that reality shows generally have as either stupid or manipulative content, many television workers are reluctant to say that they make reality TV. Instead, they often say that they make "factual entertainment" or "documentary shows" (Andersen 2018) even though the show in question easily fits the broad genre criteria for reality television (Jerslev 2014). Another way to explain this dynamic would be to say that these workers assume that it will be easier for their content to receive positive evaluations and be called creative if they use another genre label than reality. This shows that perceptions of genre can be a central part of these industry-specific logics and can have connections to industry professionals' awareness of creativity.

All media industries contain industry lore and widespread myths. Yet for many of the media professionals that I have met, the phenomenon of creativity is still one of the biggest mysteries to them and is still the subject of many long-lived industry myths. In summary, this chapter has helped to explain how there are many different challenges that you can face when you do studies of creativity in media industries.

Chapter 6

Research Design Using the Five Traditions

This chapter discusses how you can do research design when you study creativity in media industries. The purpose is to get you thinking about how *you* can research creativity in media industries and prepare you for the research process where this chapter will provide valuable insights and instructions for how you might design your study.

Before you proceed with a study of creativity in media industries, it is first crucial that you look inwards and reflect on what your own understanding of creativity is. You should ask yourself if you believe that it is possible to find, to measure and to control creativity. In order to be able to study creativity, you must be clear about how you define it and understand it. If you have read the previous chapters in the book, you have heard about the five traditions in chapter 2, which we can use in this context to look at some obvious options for research designs. The following sections will *describe how we can design a study using the respective five traditions* and discuss when it is most appropriate to use particular traditions by relating them to the characteristics of various media industries.

Individualist Research Design

As the first of the five traditions, the individualist tradition can seem both inappropriate and appropriate to use in studies of media industries. It can seem inappropriate because so many media industry practices are immensely collective team efforts where up to several hundred employees can do some kind of work on a single media production. Then it certainly sounds a bit strange to use theories from mainly psychology about individual creativity to study that team effort. However, this individualist approach might also be appropriate in our research design because we so easily could overlook the importance of each individual's influence and background in a collective process. An example of an obvious question to ask in such a study would be: To what extent do individual contributions, backgrounds, and decision-making play a crucial part in the collective media production process?

At the same time, it is relevant to discuss how the different media industries have different opportunities for one-person productions or use rather small teams. A skilled podcaster, a documentarist, or a book author can more or less do most of the work concerning production (writing, recording, editing, etc.) on their own and in principle that one person can also distribute or self-publish that same content somewhere online. Another obvious digital media semiprofessional with this kind of work process could be an influencer or vlogger who sometimes works very individually as a kind of one-person company doing business via Instagram, YouTube, or TikTok, perhaps supported and represented by a PR agency (Abidin and Ots 2016; Hearn and Schoenhoff 2015). At the other end of the scale, the less obvious media industries for individualist studies would be those with huge collective efforts such as video games, fiction films, and more production-intensive television genres. Interestingly, film and television fiction productions are usually more likely to highlight one particular individual as the primary creative force. In film, they often celebrate the director as an auteur while in television fiction they often celebrate the showrunner who is usually the principal scriptwriter. Therefore, if you are to design a research study of these media production types, you can try to swim against the stream by looking for individual creativity in other roles or "below the line" as for instance Vicky Mayer has pointed out (Mayer 2011).

Additionally, if we use some of these individualist theories about geniuses' personalities and exceptionally gifted creative practitioners, we must remember that they base many of their claims on studies of exceptionally renowned individuals that have a somewhat special and perhaps privileged position. This means that insights about how Freud, Einstein, and Picasso worked may turn out to be less telling for the everyday creative processes at, for example, an advertising agency.

As for the details of the research design, taking your inspiration from the individualist tradition can lead to the use of many different methods. While testing individuals and their personalities using quantitative scores is a popular choice in psychology, it is uncommon in media studies. Here, individual interviews, observations, and the use of, for example, participant diaries as a research method would be much more obvious methods for individualist studies in order to study how individuals experience and affect a creative process.

Sociocultural Research Design

If you take your inspiration from the second of the five traditions, the sociocultural tradition, it can lead you toward a greater awareness of the importance of the context in which creativity occurs. As a kind of countermove against the individualist tradition, the sociocultural contributions focus much more on the structures and conditions around individuals and on the assessment of creative work. Perhaps you can recall some of the insights from Amabile's works and Csikszentmihalyi's works that both stress the value of incorporating social and cultural factors such as motivations, social ties, and the evaluations of creativity.

In relation to the various media industries, the sociocultural tradition's rather generic contributions can be relevant and applicable to most of them without immediate problems. One obvious focus point would be the importance of gatekeepers and their evaluations of media work (as discussed in chapter 3), which is a dynamic we can find in most media industries. We can definitely describe some media industries as a little more exclusive and less accessible for amateurs such as film, television, and video game production—meaning that they can also have more stringent gatekeeping or require skills that are more particular and difficult to obtain. In such industries, managers and editors frequently need to say no to new ideas and people, and here it is particularly relevant to study the importance of sociocultural dynamics in how media organizations manage this exclusivity through gatekeeping, commissioning, and recruitment processes. In contrast, the podcasting industry has fewer gatekeepers (currently at least) where independent podcasters often can publish their content directly online without an editor curating or commissioning it. In this context, a primary issue for podcasters is perhaps discoverability and not as much gatekeeping or recruitment. Discoverability becomes more important for the independent content producers and, in general, it is worth studying how media platforms and content services of all kinds play an increasingly powerful role today as content curators and distributors that unnoticeably assess, rank, and situate content (van Dijck, Poell, and de Waal 2018).

That people's motivations and evaluations play an important role, is something we can study in all media industries. However, we can perhaps imagine that media organizations with very hierarchical organizational structures and large payrolls are more likely to attract workers who are motivated by those extrinsic conditions. In contrast, workers in, for example, local radio or on small and independent podcasts are more likely to have intrinsic motivations where they have a strong interest in the medium and want to practice their audio skills because they mostly just find audio work fun and fulfilling (Markman 2012).

Additionally, the research efforts about so-called creative hubs, creative clusters, or even creative cities come to mind because they stress the sociocultural importance of making industrial workspaces available where some form of creative cohabitation can happen (e.g., Hesmondhalgh 2019; Komorowski and Picone 2020; Spicer and Presence 2017). While the artistic tradition and the creative industries research field has delivered studies of these creative hubs, they have not used the lens of sociocultural creativity theory. I suggest that actual creativity theory would be interesting to apply to studies of these creative cohabitation spaces since these industry initiatives heavily imply that the space itself will make all companies involved more creative. Here we can use the sociocultural approach to question whether the label of being included in such a creative hub has any effect on the assessment of these companies' products—perhaps we can hypothesize that the primary "effect" is due to the social value of that label and not necessarily a greater creative output. The social constructivist tradition would also be obviously apt at dissecting the rhetoric around such hubs.

The biggest advantage from using the sociocultural tradition is that you get a greater awareness of how important contexts are. The message is that contextual factors such as gatekeeping, assessments, and motivations matter and that we should consider these social factors in our studies. However, one of the possible disadvantages of focusing on these contexts can perhaps be a lack of focus on the actual product.

Considering what methods we can use in sociocultural research design, the possibilities are many. However, since the sociocultural dynamics that this tradition seeks to describe are precisely social interactions between people, it seems obvious to document these dynamics by using qualitative methods such as participant observations or qualitative interviews. A comparative case study using this tradition can also be fruitful since it would then be possible to compare how two rather similar people or products have different motivations or receive contrasting assessments.

Pragmatic Research Design

The third tradition is the pragmatic and if we use that as our inspiration, we gain a lot of agency over the creative process itself and this creates some options for other kinds of research design. First, we need to adjust our mindset and not think of creativity as something uncontrollable that should be "set free" but as something malleable that we can manage and fine-tune. That general and pragmatic perspective can be relevant and applied to all kinds of creative processes and in all media industries. Second, we can apply the collectivist perspective within this tradition and take our inspiration from, for example, Sawyer and DeZutter's work where they describe group creativity as a distributed and collective phenomenon. That way of thinking is applicable when the production is a group effort, which is often the case in media industries such as television, film, radio, gaming, journalism, advertising, and so on. However, since Sawyer and DeZutter particularly study improvisation, the relevance of their insights might be greater in, for example, live productions or group situations where immediate and relatively unplanned responses are necessary. Media productions that are more individual and less group-oriented as mentioned in earlier sections are of course less obvious options to study using a pragmatic/collectivist research design.

If we fully immerse ourselves in the pragmatic tradition, we can try to remember the insights from classic design scholars like Schön and Owen. They respectively point to the importance of reflection-in-action when doing creative work and to the invention of products and the use of certain tools and materials in the creative process. As a researcher, if you try actively to seek out a group of media professionals who work in this kind of way, it should be rather straightforward to check what the theories from the pragmatic tradition say about creativity. If you do the opposite and seek out media professionals with a lower degree of creative awareness and agency, the contrast between theory and practice will naturally be much higher but then you instead have the possibility of informing them about the insights from the pragmatic tradition. Either way, the goal for the pragmatic researcher usually is to optimize the creative process and the product as much as possible in order to find out what the best practice is. In my experience, you are more likely to find practitioners with a creative awareness similar to this design-thinking approach in media organizations that recruit a large variety of workers (including design-educated workers) or that put a lot of emphasis on branding themselves as having a major creative ambition (for example organizations like LEGO).

When I look at how my colleagues in, for example, design studies usually do research, they are often not afraid to participate actively in the creative process alongside practicing professionals (see Koskinen 2011; Vaughan 2017; Cross 2006). Therefore, if you fully wish to do this kind of pragmatic research design, it seems obvious to participate and co-construct products with the practitioners you study where you can collaborate in a group on how you can best steer the process using different constraints. Another popular option is to set up an experiment and test a particular tool or exercise on a group of practitioners to learn about how they respond. If all goes well, you can possibly co-construct a product, a tool or an exercise that has value for that particular group of industry practitioners.

Another part of this tradition contains the contributions from media management that use a pragmatic approach to discuss how we at a management level can control and maximize the output of creative production processes (e.g., Davis and Scase, Bilton, or Küng). Such theories are of course relevant in studies of managers, editors, and others who have an executive role in media organizations. Just be aware that such an approach naturally takes the managers' perspective and possibly runs the risk of overlooking issues at other organizational levels due to the focus on managerial interests.

If you take your inspiration from the pragmatic approach, the general advantages are that it can deliver a sense of agency over the creative process and provides you with many generic tools, models, and exercises to study and test groups' creative work. Moreover, because these tools are generic, you can apply them to creative processes in most media industries as long as you consider how great their creative awareness actually is.

However, these tools are of course reductive and this tradition's strong and naturalized focus on such products may cause that you forget to ask particular questions or forget to take an interest in the actual individuals involved in the process. Usually, it is relevant to ask who benefits from this strong focus on optimizing products and processes—or whether the solution to a problem always is to make another product? All of these disadvantages are important to remember but perhaps it is also possible to alleviate them by combining the pragmatic tradition with insights from parts of the other four traditions.

Artistic Research Design

The fourth tradition is the artistic tradition and in contrast to the pragmatic tradition, the artistic approach will usually study what creative work looks like seen from the workers' perspective. Because this tradition has its focus on creative labor and precarious working conditions, it probably contains some of the most idealistic and normative contributions of all the five traditions. This way of doing research is inherently political and is usually skeptical of any government's efforts to instrumentalize creative industries through new political initiatives and policies.

How can we then use this interest in working conditions when we design studies of media industries? The most obvious way to go would be to use our research efforts to expose those media industries that still have poor working conditions. Yet, depending on the national context in which you conduct your study, the working conditions and the general standards of living can vary greatly. Furthermore, the transnational nature of work in media industries today and, for instance, the use of outsourcing can make working conditions more difficult to track and research. In her recent book, Sarah T. Roberts debates this particular issue in her study of how content moderation on some US-owned social media platforms is actually conducted by workers in the Philippines under rather problematic working conditions (S. T. Roberts 2019). Still, there is undoubtedly many local contexts and areas of media industries where unions have a weak position and where a more liberal perception of what constitutes reasonable labor conditions can exist. In addition, the digitalization of media industries may not be helping with these issues. An obvious area with such characteristics is influencer marketing since these workers are often one-person businesses who depend on deals with sponsors and PR agencies and whose self-employed working lives rest on their personal brand (Hearn and Schoenhoff 2015; Duffy 2015). Short-term contracts are a common condition for freelancers in many media industries and the term for this tendency is the casualization of work (Gill and Pratt 2008). Various studies of self-employed or freelance workers have shown what a work life at the margins of these industries looks like (and how gender can also affect these dynamics, see Taylor 2015) and how the creative workers today are expected to be labile and constantly ready to reinterpret their skills to new forms of work (Morgan and Nelligan 2015). Particularly precarious work or working without even getting paid is not that uncommon in these industries, which some scholars describe as "hope labor" or hopeful work (e.g., Kuehn and Corrigan 2013; Wright 2018) because the workers often hope that it will eventually lead to paid work.

What we in particular can use from this whole discussion around working conditions is the language with which these scholars describe work and give a voice to workers who are sometimes invisible or silent. In contrast, it is important for you to consider that if you choose to take your inspiration from the artistic tradition, you should think of whether you also adopt their idealistic and sometimes normative approach. For instance, if you subscribe to their general dichotomy between creativity versus commerce, there are definitely existing academic works that agree with you. Yet, that way of thinking may not result in a study that provides you with new insights about how creativity and creative processes in media industries actually work. Although it is undoubtedly important to expose poor working conditions, it is also relevant to study what those conditions actually mean for the creative output. Here it might turn out to be more valuable to combine a pragmatic and artistic approach (even if that is quite tricky) or to study and discuss what effects poor working conditions really have on media productions.

Practically speaking, some of the popular research methods in the artistic tradition are interviews, participant observations, statistics about media work and document analysis of political and strategic documents on creative industries. A particular challenge for researchers who want to conduct studies of precarious working conditions in media industries can be that some media organizations do not wish to talk about these issues. Although non-disclosure agreements (NDAs) in such a situation might create the much-needed trust between the researcher and the organization in question, the research effort can turn out to be of little value for society and the research community if you cannot publish and disseminate it. An alternative option for such a study can be to seek out the workers affected by precarious working conditions and convince them to participate in your study since they can have a strong motivation to expose these issues. Additionally, if you can track down previous employees from that particular organization, there is a good chance that they can talk more freely about the working conditions that they experienced. Of course, you should still be aware of how you can maintain validity in your study if you receive very biased accounts or only hear from disgruntled informants that, for example, were fired.

Another important contribution from the artistic tradition that can inspire us is the work around authorship. Here it can be useful to try to analyze authorship, consider the artistic dimension of a production, and discuss who should get credit for creating media products. As discussed in chapter 2, studies of literature and film have historically been important for the academic discussion of authorship and we could of course study those exact two industries. An alternative option would be to do an unusual and even trickier comparative discussion of whom the authorship belongs to in some of the more intricate or hugely collective media industries like, for example, video game productions.

In summary, there are many good reasons to apply perspectives from this diverse artistic tradition such as discussions of labor and authorship to your study of creativity in media industries. Especially the inequalities around gender, class, race, and so forth, that still to this day unfortunately characterize work in some media industries (see Conor, Gill, and Taylor 2015) provide us with a strong motivation for why this approach is valuable. That some media professionals and organizations are unwilling or afraid to discuss these issues should not stop us as long as we are mindful of the methodological and practical challenges that can transpire. Yet, you should consider whether you want your own research to become political and normative or if you prefer to stay impartial and only use some particular parts of the artistic tradition. Finally, remember not to let the interest in working conditions totally overshadow the intention to research the actual creative output since precarious production conditions might still result in some creative contributions.

Social Constructivist Research Design

The fifth and final tradition that can inspire our research designs is the social constructivist tradition. Overall, this tradition shares some of the same general skepticism toward creativity as a buzzword that we also found in the artistic tradition and has a desire to debunk the search for creativity. This of course begs the question: How can we study creativity without searching for it? Well, we can generally try to point to how media industry organizations and professionals understand, manage, and discuss creativity as a phenomenon and the myths that surround it.

When is this kind of research approach then appropriate? In most media industries, we can probably find organizations where a social constructivist case study will provide us with relevant insights about how a part of that particular industry understands creativity and creative processes. For example, you may encounter a media organization with a preference for beanbag chairs and foosball tables (table football) that perhaps even has words like "creative" and "creativity" written on their walls. We can understand such items as artifacts and the words as espoused values that represent the organizational culture (Schein 1985). One particular area where I have seen this exact kind of organizational culture, where they appear to be celebrating creativity, is at advertising agencies, but we can probably find similar examples in most media industries.

If we, as researchers, focus on the discourses around creativity instead of searching for creativity itself, it gives us the possibility of analyzing and dissecting the language and narratives with which these industry organizations and informants describe the phenomenon (inspired by Taylor 2013). This approach can also be useful for student projects to counteract those situations where students are tempted just to describe how creative their informants are, which can result in a simple and superficial analysis. The social constructivist approach can then be a tool that forces them to look beyond the superficial talk about creativity and to reflect on *why* the informants talk about their work in this way (e.g., what motivates the informants' discourse).

Another option when we work with the social constructivist tradition is to focus on whether there are any negative consequences in cases where these industries focus heavily on being creative or maximizing their creative output. Previously, this way of thinking inspired some of my own research efforts. In those studies, I found the idea of creativity possibly having negative dimensions quite thought provoking. Is this a part of creativity that we sometimes tend to ignore? As mentioned earlier, the desire to maximize creativity can put pressure on developers and production teams in media industries. Discourses about creativity can contain many expectations and it can sometimes be difficult to live up to these. At times, we can feel disappointed in creative processes due to our own expectations for how creative we expected to be (perhaps you have also experienced this yourself). However, I will state that I currently work more by combining the five traditions and not solely with the social constructivist approach.

This aspect of creativity about disappointment and failure is usually not on the agenda in studies of media industries even though it could lead to relevant and interesting findings in my opinion. One obvious reason why few study this is that media organizations often prefer to mention their success stories instead of discussing their failed projects or the productions that disappointed them—even though we might all learn a lot from such cases. Plenty of media productions fail or managers somehow perceive them as failures and this dynamic can vary depending on the form of media production. In the media industries with many fast production processes such as news journalism or podcasting, we can hypothesize that there is more room for failure and lower expectations due to the high tempo and the amount of content produced. In contrast, we know that, for example, video game and film productions have quite few and quite slow production processes, which can make failure a much bigger issue for the production company since there is longer time for everyone to build high expectations—and since a large sum of money depends on one production's success or failure. However, we definitely need more studies of perceptions of failures, disappointments, and creative expectations in various media industries to check these hypotheses.

As a final option in this tradition, our studies can choose to analyze how media professionals perceive themselves and how they construct their professional identity. In chapter 2, I mentioned the works of Stephanie Taylor and others in this area, which is inspired by social psychology (Taylor and Littleton 2012; Taylor and Luckman 2020). The inherently social constructivist part of this approach to identity is that it comes with an understanding of these professional identities as complex, ambiguous, and socially constructed. Such an approach can illuminate why creative workers can have many different and at times contradictory identifications when they talk about who they are and what they work with. By focusing on the informants' own narratives, we can avoid defining creativity for them and we can highlight their own definitions of what being creative means. This is a research approach that we can apply to any workers in any media industries in order to learn more about their self-perceptions.

For this social constructivist tradition, there are many options when it comes to research designs and research methods but the primary focus is usually on the social aspects and the narrative-discursive aspects. This means that we can conduct observations of social settings, workspaces, and work cultures. This can tell us a lot about the social negotiations that exist around the employees and the productions. We can conduct interviews with creative professionals about the self-perceptions and do discourse analysis of these data sources. On top of that, we can choose to study how these self-perceptions change over time and throughout creative professionals' careers. Finally, we can even try to gather data about failed projects and negative consequences of creativity, where we can use surveys, focus groups, quantitative studies and so on.

In summary, the social constructivist tradition has various offerings for those researchers who perhaps are getting a little tired of all that talk about creativity and instead want to dissect these discourses or turn the concept upside down and focus on the negative parts. The primary challenge within this way of working is that it can maybe add to the confusion over what creativity is. If we choose to embrace the total antiessentialism in this social constructivist approach, creativity is nothing at all and has no essence. If you find that too tiring, then you can choose to merely use parts of this fifth tradition in your research design or to disregard it entirely.

Using and Combining Different Traditions, Designs and Methods

As a final recommendation for studies of creativity in media industries, I wish to recap what my initial intention is behind the five traditions as a theoretical framework. The most optimal way to use what this book can teach you would be to try to consider all five traditions when you study creativity. Use the best parts of them and see what they can contribute within your study. Instead of committing to just one of the five traditions and ignoring the other four, I recommend that you combine several traditions when you design and conduct your study. Similarly, you can choose to combine and mix several different methods as well in order to gain various different perspectives on these industries' creative processes.

For example, in that kind of case study, you can start with a quantitative analysis of what the creative output from your object of study actually contains (as mentioned in chapter 5). If you study this over time or create a yearly overview, you gain valuable key figures that give you an excellent starting point by outlining what your object of study is and has been in recent years. Subsequently, such a quantitative overview can work well in combination with later qualitative studies.

Based on the previous chapters, we can identify several obvious questions that we can ask in most case studies about creativity. Therefore, as a way of wrapping up this chapter about research design, I give you this *short list of helpful questions* that you can use as a possible inspiration when you design your study:

- What is their creative output (e.g., in key figures)?
- How great is their creative awareness (do they find themselves able to control, evaluate, or reflect on creative processes)?
- What do individual contributions and group dynamics mean for their creative process?
- What is necessary for a production in that particular media industry to be labelled as creative—and who decides that?

- How do these media professionals and organizations use the label of creativity and why do they use it?
- What is their creative self-perception and how do they understand their own professional role?
- Why is this an important case in media industries and what do we learn about creativity by studying it?

Chapter 7

Case Example

Where Is Creativity in TV Production?

This seventh chapter provides a case example to make the dynamics in creative processes more tangible for you as readers. My example is television production and I draw on my experiences from a production study where I researched a Danish television channel (in 2016–2019) as well as from other various encounters with the television industry. You can find my other publications about that study if you want to know more about the details (Andersen 2019a, b), but in this chapter I will tell a more general version of the events. I will use this fieldwork to consider *where we can go in a television preproduction process to "see creativity."* The case example will demonstrate how the creative processes behind media products are often collective, complex, and ambiguous.

During this fieldwork, I observed and interviewed different employees at two internal youth departments at the Danish public-service television network DR. The first department was their youth TV channel DR3 and the second department was the internal youth content production department DR Ung. In order to narrow down the scope of my fieldwork, I chose to focus on their preproduction and idea development processes. I did on-off observations of them for several months where I regularly attended meetings in/between these two departments and observed idea development sessions and pitch meetings. In the following 12 months, I then interviewed four different editors from both departments and two freelance employees about their strategic approaches to, for example, idea development and their creative awareness in order to identify how they understood creativity in television production. To be clear, I understand the preproduction phase as a key part of television production even though these early stages are not always as popular to study as the later on-set production phase.

In the following sections, I will discuss how the preproduction phase (and the later phases) consists of a multitude of underlying processes that may contain elements of so-called creativity. The goal is to show how complex creativity and media productions are in order to discuss why the key to increasing our creativity seems to be so elusive.

Conditions in the Pre-Production Phase

Initially, it is important to stress that before anyone has done anything in pre-production and idea development, the preexisting conditions and constraints are already in play. The editors have established a personal taste and the developers or program planners perhaps have some kind of knowledge—their discerned savvy (Draper 2014)—about what the editors' tastes have been up until now. This means that even though no one has said anything about this new round of idea development, these preexisting conditions have already narrowed down the realm of possible ideas (or design space).

Then the channel sends out *the briefs*. As we discussed in chapter 3, briefs are short summaries that outline what the idea development processes need to deliver. In this case, the upper management in DR had chosen some strategic focus areas and in cooperation with the channel's editorial team, they created 12 different briefs asking for many different kinds of programming ideas. These briefs naturally limit the possibilities even further while also delivering a number of themes from which to develop new ideas. Are these briefs then examples of creativity? They definitely frame and situate the creative process that follows and they certainly play an important role later in the idea development sessions. Of course, the briefs do not totally guarantee that you will only receive ideas within the mentioned themes. Yet, in the processes I observed, everyone seemed very keen on delivering exactly what briefs asked for. However, one major issue was that the briefs—and in particular one brief called "DR3's next big experiment"—asked for *radically creative ideas* that went beyond the brief. These ambitious and still vague briefs were confusing to the developers. Because how do you go beyond the brief (and beyond your editors' tastes) and maximize your creativity when you usually navigate after these gatekeepers' tastes and opinions? As the following sections will illustrate, this was perhaps too difficult a mission for the developers.

Observing Idea Development

A couple of days before the first idea development session, the two departments held a joint meeting about the briefs. This was to aid the rather confused developers who struggled with how they were supposed to interpret the briefs. Again, the channel editors stressed that the developers were welcome to pitch some radical and crazy ideas that went across genres and beyond the briefs. My interpretation of this dynamic was that this exchange created high expectations in both departments for what level of creativity the idea development sessions should deliver.

Then the developers met in a small group of 5 to 10 people for two working days of *idea development sessions*. As a kind of tool in the process, they had decided to leave their normal workplace and meet at a nearby venue with small meeting rooms. We can interpret this "going away" as a sort of tool in itself, which can symbolize how they wanted to move away from their usual work patterns. Once the actual brainstorming sessions started, they kept using the briefs as starting points for the group's discussion of all their ideas (e.g., "now we are discussing ideas for brief no. 1," etc.). In this phase, there were definitely situations where the idea development was similar to Sawyer and DeZutter's distributed and collective creation process, where everyone in this collective contributed to the creation by giving immediate responses and reiterations of each other's ideas. Is this distributed creation of ideas then the pinnacle of creativity or do we just perceive it like that? For this group of developers, it seemed like they enjoyed sharing their ideas with the rest of the group and cooperating on developing them. The fact that no one really knows what the outcome of that kind of brainstorming will be can also make it more exciting to take part in.

After these collective brainstorming sessions, the group split up into two or sometimes three smaller groups. As I mentioned in chapter 3 about how to observe creativity, this put me as a researcher in a dilemma. Whom should I then follow? Where and when was the creativity or the big breakthrough going to "happen"? After some time I accepted how it would be impossible for me to oversee all these simultaneous sessions and tried to make peace with that.

Throughout these two days, they developed many different ideas, mostly by adding small and incremental changes little by little. Only once or twice did they come up with some kind of big breakthrough where they developed a strong idea very quickly, so if I am to make an accurate description of these events, the small and incremental processes definitely seemed more frequent and prevalent.

Struggling With Creative Processes

In general, there definitely were some challenges for this group of developers. Their biggest challenge was probably that they struggled to live up to their own expectations. When the two days were done, I asked some of the lead developers about how it went and they were *not* satisfied with what they had delivered as a group so far. In addition, there still were some briefs that they had not developed any ideas for—and the unclear brief about the next big experiment was one of them. Because of this lackluster feeling, they decided to arrange one more day of idea development sessions and again they went away to another location. This time they chose a local fairground (probably because it seemed like a fun and creative location), ordered some traditional dishes and had a beer. That day, they even tried a little post-it exercise that they had once learned at the journalism school. Still, they never found an idea in these sessions that lived up to the expectations that the experiment brief had helped create.

One can wonder if their expectations were too high or if their performance was too poor. When I asked the developers, they thought that their ideas were definitely not as creative as they had hoped. Of course, the expectations created by the ambitious briefs probably affected their responses. From my observations of these sessions, it was also clear that they saw creativity and idea development as something uncontrollable. The just did it and did not really reflect-in-action or discuss their own process while brainstorming. Even though they tried to use the locations and the post-it exercise as tools, my experience was that they struggled with how they should respond when creativity did not occur organically during these idea development sessions. As the following weeks demonstrated, idea development is not something that necessarily only happens during the few hours where you allocate time for brainstorming. In reality, they kept developing most of their ideas over a much longer period of several months.

Because of all these considerations, I dare to say that the developers and editors' creative awareness was somewhat weak. When I later interviewed some of the editors, I definitely got the impression that these two departments still had a romantic perception of creativity as something that needed to be "set free" and not a pragmatic understanding of it as something we can manage by using tools or by self-imposing constraints.

Another remarkable thing about the idea development was that the developers regularly discussed whether an idea matched with the editors' tastes and preferences. Yet, the developers never mentioned whether an idea would match the audience's taste (at least not while I was observing them). Although this was surprising to me, one explanation may be that the task of ensuring that programs would fit the preferences of the channel's target group was the channel editors' responsibility and not the developers'.

Pitching and Selecting Ideas for Production

Once the developers had narrowed down their pools of ideas and selected a few for each brief, they began to prepare their *pitching sessions*. First, they had to pitch to the editors in their own department. Second, they had to pitch to the channel editors a few weeks later who made the final decision about which ideas to commission.

For these pitching sessions that took place in a small meeting room, they prepared slideshows to fit each brief and each pitching session focused on two briefs at once. For example, for the briefs about dating and about the next big experiment, they had one slideshow with four ideas for dating shows and three ideas for experiments. The surprising thing to me was that these slideshows were rather vague and for instance used only stock photos in order to keep the pitch open for interpretation. The developers then explained to me that if they had used, for example, a picture of a recognizable media persona as the host, it could seem like they had already chosen that one host as the "face" of the idea. When the developers then pitched their ideas, they often included blank spaces (figuratively speaking) and made room for the editors to make suggestions. This allowed editors to cocreate and alter suggested ideas and, for the developers, it ensured that a particular idea still had a chance to progress even though the editors wanted to change it to some extent. We could describe this creative dynamic as a form of cocreation but I believe that this actually was more of a gatekeeping dynamic that demonstrated the distribution of power between developers and editors. I also observed pitching sessions with external production companies, which overall were rather similar except that they were slightly more formal and took place in a larger meeting room.

Then came the time where the channel editors had to *select ideas* that they wanted to commission. This was a very tangible example of how these editors conducted their role as gatekeepers. Unfortunately, they did not allow me to observe the editorial meeting where they chose which ideas to commission. Yet, they were kind enough to share their spreadsheet with me where they had written down all suggested ideas and their decisions. In total, the channel editors received 98 ideas. Sixty-six of those ideas received a "no," 30 ideas received a "maybe" and they only commissioned two ideas for production. That adds up to *a success rate of approximately 2 percent*. Although, some of the rejected ideas did return in later development rounds and got approval. In this round, both of the approved ideas were internal—one about a dating/travel show and one about swinger clubs. Based on that, it is fair to say that the task of rejecting ideas was a big part of the channel editors' job and that the ideas they chose did not really match the briefs' desire for maximum creativity and radical experiments (in my assessment at least). While the swinger club idea definitely matched the channel's brand, there had already been other Danish television programs about swinger clubs so it was hardly a never-before-seen idea. The more interesting aspect of it was that when the developers came up with that swinger idea, they all instantly agreed that this was a perfect match for the editors' taste—and they were right! The dating and travel idea was also very similar to some of DR3's existing programs about those themes. Therefore, both of these looked like risk-adverse choices to some extent.

To me, this was an ambiguous outcome of the whole idea development process. On the one hand, it made me wonder whether the bold and ambitious language in the briefs was perhaps mostly something the editors liked to say but not what they actually wanted or what the developers could deliver in the end. On the other hand, it made me think that the initial expectations had been high and that this had put a substantial pressure on the developers who seemed slightly stressed out during these weeks. Concerning their working conditions, the channel had little money and many of the developers had short-term contracts, so they were also just trying to secure their own contract renewal by getting ideas approved. The presence of these structural constraints (which of course can be productive as well) probably added to the overall pressure.

To summarize it all, even though the editors had tried to tell the developers to be radical, original, and go beyond the brief, the idea development was still mostly a matter of pleasing those editors and their tastes. This leads me to this chapter's final section on where creativity is in the preproduction phase of television.

Where was the Creativity Then?

I chose to study the idea development phase because I expected to find the explanation of how creativity happens in television production. Rather than finding the pinnacle of television creativity, I think that I found an explanation for why radical creativity is often difficult to achieve within the structural conditions of the television industry. This was supposed to be the experimental youth channel. Rather, it turned out to be a case that demonstrated how the reality in media industries every so often is that "nobody dares" as I discussed in chapter 3. Risk-adverse behavior is understandable especially for media professionals with precarious working conditions. They fear the risk of the production failing and what that might mean to their careers and we can probably find this risk-adverse behavior in many media industries.

Of course, idea development is not the only phase in television production where some kind of creative process takes place. Yet, as this case example demonstrates, we can use studies of idea development to find some important insights about how channel editors and developers understand, manage, and mismanage creative processes. I ended my fieldwork after the idea selection phase because I had already gathered more than enough data, but, in general, the following phases could prove to be revealing as well.

In terms of all the other key creative processes in television, *casting* is usually an important phase in the production of both fiction and factual content.

Even though casting is typically a closed process where few researchers are welcome (e.g., Mayer 2013; Wyatt and Bunton 2012), studying it can give us insights about how the production team negotiates the clash between an imagined cast and an actual cast, which may require a lot of creative rethinking from the production team. Once the actual *shooting* process begins on-set, it can again generate the need for creative alterations along the way. The many sunk costs of a potentially expensive production process can make shooting a stressful phase with many long days and unexpected changes for the workers involved. We should also consider the importance of the *editing* phase where they create the final story lines and where they often need to process and look through many hours of recorded content in order to arrive at a product that fits the client's needs (either the channel or streaming service).

All of these phases can contain creative decision-making. The perceived creativity of a television production may even change after airing. In another case study of Danish youth fiction series (Andersen 2017), it was clear that the channel's editorial team found the final series to be rather disappointing and not that creative. However, their opinions changed when the reviews and the audience ratings came in. Then they suddenly altered their narrative and started describing the series as a "surprising success." What if that series had not succeeded in changing the editors' minds? Or the audience's minds? Or the reviewers' minds? This tells us that the perceived creative value of a media product like a television program is not set in stone but is socially negotiable and can change over time.

I hope that this case example and my discussion of it has illustrated how there are many collective, complex, and ambiguous social dynamics within the creative processes that take place in media industries. Depending on which of the five traditions we use, we can claim that creativity is present in many of these different production phases. Perhaps these complex dynamics explain why we generally experience creativity as something strange and elusive. At this point, my best bet is that if we use all five traditions and their nuanced ways of understanding creativity as a phenomenon, we stand a much better chance of decoding its complexities. By adopting these different ways of understanding it, we can hope that we will eventually find it easier to explain, analyze, and manage creativity.

Chapter 8

Further Studies of Creativity in Media Industries

The previous chapters have focused on what we know about creativity in media industries at this point. This concluding chapter will focus on what we do *not* know about it yet and on what we still need to study. First, I will highlight some of the main points from the other chapters to set the scene before I proceed to pinpoint areas that need further research.

The Book's Main Points

As the first chapter has pointed out, if we are to study creativity and use it as a term, we need to define more precisely in order to have a stable concept to work with. The introduction stated precisely how this book's purpose is to *bring together contributions from the cross-disciplinary field of creativity research and to highlight the insights that can benefit research in media industry studies*. This purpose connects to my claim about how only a few media scholars are aware of the many important and relevant contributions from actual creativity research. I hope that this book will encourage more of my colleagues and students to take an interest in creativity research since creativity looks like a persistent topic that continues to be on the societal agenda.

The second chapter has then facilitated this much-needed theoretical and cross-disciplinary discussion by creating an overview of literature from the vast field of creativity research. By presenting the five traditions, each of which represents a particular way of understanding creativity, I have created a framework and a tool that I hope can aid students and fellow researchers who seek to understand the concept of creativity.

The third chapter has presented key concepts and discussions in media industry studies around related themes such as autonomy, idea development, gatekeeping and Caves's concept of nobody knows. In relation to that, I have suggested that the issue is not that nobody knows but that media industries' organizational structures encourage risk reduction and often reward small and incremental innovations rather than radical ones—which is why a more precise description might be "nobody dares."

The fourth chapter has pointed to some of the general challenges when we do production studies concerning access negotiations, data collection, and how time can affect your production study. I highlight productions studies as a methodological approach because I find that it is demanding but valuable to us as researchers as long as we reflect on the challenges that can transpire.

The fifth chapter has focused on the particular challenges that can occur when you do a study of creativity. In that context, we have discussed where creativity is and where it probably is not, how we can handle the challenge of normativity and how to document creativity. We have also discussed the challenges of working with qualitative and quantitative methods and how we can be mindful of industry-specific logics and genre perceptions. In connection to that, I launched my concept of creative awareness defined as informants' self-reflexivity about their actions in creative processes and their understanding of what creativity is.

The sixth chapter has given a number of suggestions for different research designs that you can use to study creativity based on the five traditions and their approaches to the concept. In the end of that chapter, I encouraged you to combine and mix the five traditions and I have provided a list of questions that you can use as an inspiration in your own research design.

The seventh and second-to-last chapter has recounted events from my fieldwork when I studied a Danish television channel's idea development processes. I have used those experiences as a case example to show where we can go in a television preproduction process to "see creativity." As that case has illustrated, we can describe many of those subprocesses in media production as creative, and yet, the outcome of the idea development itself was disappointing to the two departments involved. That case has provided us with demonstrations of the importance of gatekeepers' tastes and of how creative processes can be collective, complex, and socially ambiguous. It has also shown how some media professionals can have a romantic understanding of creativity and sometimes can even give up on trying to manage it.

Suggestions for Further Studies

After establishing what we know, we can now ask how we can proceed from here. What kind of studies could contribute with useful ideas and where are the gaps in the current body of literature? Naturally, this is difficult to say with total precision and of course, my claims here connect to my own preferences and favorite topics.

With that in mind, I will say first that we need more studies that compare the creative processes in different media industries. Not only do the respective research areas of media industry studies and creativity research function as separate fields without much comparison but we could also use more comparative work that links different media industries with each other. Much of the research in media industries is isolated within a particular medium with the risk of being overlooked by other media researchers. To me at least, creative processes in media industries can serve as an obvious topic under which we can compare these industries. Another obvious topic could be streaming and how digitalization affects various media industries, which I have also written about recently (Andersen and Lüders 2021). We, of course, already have quite a few studies of these topics but usually only within one medium and only a few researchers have tried to compare how these developments unfold in several media industries at once (Colbjørnsen 2020; Herbert, Lotz, and Marshall 2019; Sundet and Colbjørnsen 2021). In the context of creativity, more comparative studies of streaming within different media industries could reveal how the publishing strategies on these streaming services and their need for content may affect their content production and thereby their creative processes. It would be interesting to me at least to know more about how streaming can have an impact on how organizations from various media industries approach their creative processes and idea development.

Since I am broadly interested in many kinds of media, I am also curious to know more about creative processes in those media industries that do not always receive the same attention as others do. My academic career started in a research environment where television studies had a quite strong position and long-running tradition, which is why I have been able to hear and learn much about that particular industry. However, there are definitely media industries that we as scholars hear less about (depending on where we work). For me, the neglected industries have been particularly the video game industry and to some degree the podcasting industry and the advertising industry. Fortunately, there has recently been conducted relevant studies of the dynamics within the video game industry (e.g., Kerr 2017; Ozimek 2018; Sotamaa and Švelch 2021), the podcasting industry (e.g., Berry 2016; Markman 2012; Spinelli and Dann 2019), and the advertising industry (e.g., Fill, Hughes, and De Francesco 2013; Sherman 2020), but not with a focus on creative processes, regrettably.

Tentative Hypotheses About Creativity in Media Industries

Throughout the book, I have presented some of my hypotheses about what the logics and patterns in various kinds of media production can mean for their understanding of creative processes. We can characterize the first group of media as *the long forms of production* in media industries. This group includes the production of video games, film, and certain television genres that all can have long and continuous processes of production and development. They are domains with a low accessibility, high starting costs, expensive technical equipment and high skill requirements, which may mean that they innovate and change at a slower pace (McIntyre, Fulton, and Paton 2016, 33). The second group contains *the short forms of production* in media industries. This group includes the production of news journalism and certain radio genres and podcast productions. These domains are more accessible, have medium-to-low starting costs, cheaper technical equipment and medium-to-low skill requirements. My underlying assumption in this distinction is logically that the media forms within the same group probably share similar ways of understanding and managing creativity because the pace and duration of their production processes are somewhat similar. However, I really want to stress that this is only a tentative hypotheses that I would like to investigate further in the future and that I welcome others to challenge. Outside or in between these two groups we have industries like advertising, social media, music, and so forth, which can produce content at different paces and durations and they are therefore more difficult to place. Previously, other scholars have also tried to divide the media industries or cultural industries into various categories (e.g., Miège 1989), which is notoriously tricky to do in a neat and orderly fashion.

Particularly, I wish to use my two suggested groups of media industries (the long vs. short forms of production) to point to the challenges that the much-needed comparative studies of media industries probably can encounter. First, it is not a given that these respective industries (or the scholars that study them) will appreciate comparative and cross-industrial findings. Such findings might actually challenge industry-specific understandings and point to the need for changes, which is not necessarily what media companies and professionals always want to hear. Second, we as researchers may experience that it is difficult to adapt to either the long or the short pace and duration of these productions when we conduct production studies—not to mention the challenge of studying more than one kind of industry at the same time. For instance, if you want to study and document a single production from start to finish in the video game industry, you will probably have to spend several years in order to do so. In comparison, if you want to do the same with a single production in news journalism, you risk missing it completely if you hesitate just for a day or two.

Specific *media genres* can also contain certain conditions and logics to which you may need to adapt, and in particular, we can find major differences between fiction and factual productions not only in television and radio

(Bruun and Frandsen 2017, 122) but also in other media industries. This area concerning genres and creativity is highly interesting to me since very few have dared to connect these two concepts. In chapter 5, I mentioned genres as creative constraints that both limit and enable creativity. Another point about genres concerns the high or low status that certain genres can have, where I have mentioned reality television as a genre to which some television professionals do not want to be associated. The reason is probably that they expect that their productions will get more praise for being creative if they use a different genre label such as factual television. Based on these considerations in the television industry, I hypothesize that perceptions of genre can be a central part of industry-specific logics and can have connections to industry professionals' creative awareness. Nonetheless, there are still certain circumstances about genres that seem slightly puzzling to me as a creativity researcher. If we consider that an industry professional's goal sometimes is to deliver radically creative content, I would expect to see much more daring media content with unconventional genre configurations than we currently do. What actually occurs in many cases is that content producers crowd around some of the same genres. Why is that? Havens and Lotz point to the media industries' need for risk reduction and their hopes of reaching a stable and genre-faithful audience (Havens and Lotz 2016, 14). While it is understandable and plausible that strategic considerations and fears of financial ruin may govern these industries' genre usage, it would still be relevant to study whether this is actually the case and why few dare to bet on radical creativity. I suggest that this may even have some connections to the following section about creative failure and disappointment.

Studies of Creative Failure and Disappointment

As I have touched upon throughout the book and particularly in chapter 6, we could probably find useful insights if we did more studies of creative failure and disappointment in media industries. This topic is something I have been reflecting on for some time and I believe both media scholars and organizations can benefit from more openly discussing perceived failures where involved parties or stakeholders express disappointment over the final production. We can possibly even connect this topic to my previous concepts of the long versus the short forms of production and *consider how the pace and duration of these forms of production can create different levels of creative expectations*. If we pour a lot of time into a project, is it then possible that we care more about whether it succeeds or not? To follow this line of thought, this suggests that, for example, a failed video game is much more expensive and damaging to a media company than a failed news article. If we continue this comparison, there will usually be much higher creative expectations for a video game than for a news article and thus higher disappointment. That we rarely hear of "failed news articles" is probably because no one cares about them. Those articles still fulfill their role of filling up the pages and blank spaces in order to publish a full edition of a newspaper or news webpage.

That so much media content in general fails or is lost and forgotten is both scary and fascinating to me. I partly base the above-mentioned claims on the fieldwork that I presented in chapter 7. In that, I have described how the editors initially rejected 98% of the suggested ideas. Even when the ideas do become television programs, they still risk falling into oblivion. However, if we are to study these cases to a higher extent, we need to get the media industry organizations and informants to participate in these discussions. Disappointment and failure is usually not something they want to talk about even though it could lead to relevant and interesting findings in my opinion. To summarize, I stress the need for more studies of perceptions of creative failures, disappointments, and expectations in various media industries to gain insights into the social constructivist dynamics around media productions as creative processes.

Creative Labor and Working Conditions

As a final suggestion, I point to the discussion of precarious working conditions. In previous chapters, I have had some quarrels with the parts of the creative industries and creative labor literature that apply a one-sided approach to studies of working conditions. To summarize my earlier comments on this topic, my intention is by no means to trivialize poor working conditions or to deny their existence. Rather, one of this book's intentions is to show how their political objective to defend the workers has led some scholars to neglect defining creativity as a phenomenon in itself.

Because of this, I want to encourage more studies of how particular working conditions affect creative processes. We know by now that media industries contain tendencies like, for example, casualization, outsourcing or "crunch" periods where you work perhaps 60 hours or more per week before the release of, for example, a new video game (Havens and Lotz 2016, 167). While we could of course try to defend workers against such tendencies, we could also conduct studies of it. What does the amount of working hours mean in creative industries? What kind of creative process do, for example, periods of "crunch" work generate and what kinds of creative awareness and expectations exist there?

I hope that this book can lead more researchers, students, and professionals in media industry studies and creative industries to become curious about creativity as a phenomenon. As I said in the beginning, this book will not make you more creative. Instead, I hope that it will give you the aspiration to analyze, criticize, and research how creativity works in media industries today.

References

Abidin, Crystal, and Mart Ots. 2016. Influencers tell all? Unravelling authenticity and credibility in a brand scandal. In *Blurring the Lines: Market-Driven and Democracy-Driven Freedom of Expression*, edited by Maria Edström, Andrew T. Kenyon, and Eva-Maria Svensson, 153–61. Gothenburg: Nordicom.

Alačovska, Ana. 2013. Creativity in the brief: Travel guidebook writers and good work. In *Exploring Creativity: Evaluative Practices in Innovation, Design, and the Arts*, edited by Bo T. Christensen and Brian Moeran, 172–90. Cambridge: Cambridge University Press.

Altheide, David L., and Robert P. Snow. 1979. *Media logic*, Sage library of social research; vol. 89. Beverly Hills, CA: Sage Publications.

Alvarado, Manuel, and Edward Buscombe. 1978. *Hazell: The making of a TV series*. London: British Film Institute.

Amabile, Teresa M. 1983. The social psychology of creativity: A componential conceptualization. *Journal of Personality and Social Psychology* 45 (2): 357–76.

Amabile, Teresa M. 1996. *Creativity in context*. Boulder, CO: Westview Press.

Amabile, Teresa M., Regina Conti, Heather Coon, Jeffrey Lazenby, and Michael Herron. 1996. Assessing the work environment for creativity. *The Academy of Management Journal* 39 (5): 1154–84. doi: 10.2307/256995.

Andersen, Mads Møller. 2017. Negotiating creativity on a small budget: Creative assumptions in DR3's TV commissioning. *Nordicom* Review 39 (1): 19–32.

Andersen, Mads Møller Tommerup. 2018. DR3 på flow og streaming—en todelt kanalanalyse [DR3 on flow and streaming—A two-tiered channel analysis]. *MedieKultur: Journal of Media and Communication Research* 34 (65): 138–57.

Andersen, Mads Møller Tommerup. 2019a. *DR3 og det kreative pres*. Aarhus University: AU Library/AU Fællestrykkeriet.

Andersen, Mads Møller Tommerup. 2019b. Gatekeeping within the simplicity regime: Evaluative practices in television idea development. *Media, Culture & Society*. doi: 10.1177/0163443719867300.

Andersen, Mads Møller Tommerup, and Marika Lüders. 2021. Streaming media: Production, interfaces, content and users. *MedieKultur: Journal of Media and Communication Research* 37 (70): 1–11. doi: 10.7146/mediekultur.v37i70.126152.

Appadurai, Arjun. 1986. *The social life of things: Commodities in cultural perspective*. Cambridge: Cambridge University Press.
Bakøy, Eva, Roel Puijk, and Andrew Spicer. 2017. *Building successful and sustainable film and television businesses: A cross-national perspective*. Bristol, UK: Intellect.
Banks, Mark. 2007. *The politics of cultural work*. Basingstoke: Palgrave Macmillan.
Banks, Mark. 2017. *Creative justice: Cultural industries, work and inequality*. Lanham, MD: Rowman & Littlefield International.
Banks, Miranda J., Bridget Conor, and Vicki Mayer. 2015. *Production studies, the sequel! Cultural studies of global media industries*. New York: Routledge.
Barron, Frank. 1955. The disposition towards originality. *Journal of Abnormal and Social Psychology* 51: 478.
Barthes, Roland, ed. 2004. *Forfatterens død og andre essays, Moderne tænkere*. Kbh.: Gyldendal.
Batty, Craig, Marsha Berry, Kath Dooley, Bettina Frankham, and Susan Kerrigan. 2019. *The Palgrave handbook of screen production*. Cham: Springer International Publishing AG.
Batty, Craig, and Susan Kerrigan. 2018. *Screen production research: Creative practice as a mode of enquiry*. Cham, Switzerland: Springer International Publishing AG.
Becker, Howard Saul. 1982. *Art worlds*. Berkeley, CA: University of California Press.
Berry, Richard. 2016. Podcasting: Considering the evolution of the medium and its association with the word "radio." *Radio journal* 14 (1): 7–22. doi: 10.1386/rjao.14.1.7_1.
Bilton, Chris. 2007. *Management and creativity: From creative industries to creative management*. Malden, MA: Blackwell Pub.
Bilton, Chris. 2013. Playing to the gallery: Myth method and complexity in the creative process. In *Handbook of Research on Creativity*, edited by Kerry Thomas, 559. Cheltenham, UK: Edward Elgar.
Bilton, Chris. 2015. Uncreativity: The shadow side of creativity. *International Journal of Cultural Policy* 21 (2): 153–67.
Bilton, Chris, and Stephen Cummings. 2010. *Creative strategy: Reconnecting business and innovation*. Chichester, UK: John Wiley & Sons, Ltd.
Biskjær, Michael Mose. 2013. *Self-Imposed creativity constraints*. Aarhus: Aarhus University.
Biskjær, Michael Mose, and Kim Halskov. 2014. Decisive constraints as a creative resource in interaction design. *Digital Creativity* 25 (1): 27–61. doi: 10.1080/14626268.2013.855239.
Boden, Margaret A. 1990. *The creative mind: Myths & mechanisms*. New York: Basic Books.
Bourdieu, Pierre. 1977. *Outline of a theory of practice*. Cambridge studies in social anthropology; 16. Cambridge: Cambridge University Press.
Bourdieu, Pierre. 1984. *Distinction: A social critique of the judgement of taste*. London: Routledge & Kegan Paul.
Bourdieu, Pierre. 1990. *The logic of practice*. Cambridge: Polity.

Bourdieu, Pierre. 1993. *The field of cultural production: Essays on art and literature, European perspektives*. New York: Columbia University Press.
Bourdieu, Pierre. 1996. *The rules of art: Genesis and structure of the literary field*. Cambridge: Polity Press.
Bruhn Jensen, Klaus. 2002. *A handbook of media and communication research: Qualitative and quantitative methodologies*. New York: Routledge.
Bruun, Hanne. 2011. Genre in media production. *MedieKultur: Journal of Media and Communication Research* 27 (51): 22–39.
Bruun, Hanne. 2014. Eksklusive Informanter: Om forskningsinterviewet som redskab i produktionsanalysen. *N O R D I C O M - Information* 36 (1): 29–45.
Bruun, Hanne, and Kirsten Frandsen. 2017. Tid og timing: Et metodisk perspektiv på produktionsanalyse. *MedieKultur: Journal of Media and Communication Research* 33 (62): 119–33. doi.org/10.7146/mediekultur.v33i62.25217.
Buccafusco, Christopher, and Christopher Jon Sprigman. 2011. The creativity effect. *University of Chicago Law Review* 78 (1): 31–52.
Caldwell, John Thornton. 2008. *Production culture: Industrial reflexivity and critical practice in film and television*. Durham, NC: Duke University Press.
Caves, Richard E. 2000. *Creative industries: Contracts between art and commerce*. Cambridge, MA: Harvard University Press.
Colbjørnsen, Terje. 2020. The streaming network: Conceptualizing distribution economy, technology, and power in streaming media services. *Convergence,* October 2020. doi: 10.1177/1354856520966911.
Conor, Bridget. 2010. "Everybody's a writer": Theorizing screenwriting as creative labour. *Journal of Screenwriting* 1 (1): 27.
Conor, Bridget, Rosalind Gill, and Stephanie Taylor. 2015. Gender and creative labour. *The Sociological Review* 63 (1): 1–22.
Cottle, Simon. 2007. Ethnography and news production: New(s) developments in the field. *Sociology Compass* 1 (1): 1–16. doi: 10.1111/j.1751-9020.2007.00002.x.
Coughlan, Tim, and Peter Johnson. 2008. Idea management in creative lives. CHI '08 Extended Abstracts on Human Factors in Computing Systems, Florence, Italy.
Cropley, David H., Arthur J. Cropley, James C. Kaufman, and Mark A. Runco. 2010. *The dark side of creativity*. New York: Cambridge University Press.
Cross, Nigel. 2006. *Designerly ways of knowing*. London: Springer.
Csikszentmihalyi, Mihaly. 1988. Society, culture, and person: A systems view of creativity. In *The Nature of Creativity: Contemporary Psychological Perspectives*, edited by Robert J. Sternberg, 325–39. Cambridge: Cambridge University Press.
Csikszentmihalyi, Mihaly. 1997. *Creativity: Flow and the psychology of discovery and invention*. New York: Harper Perennial.
Csikszentmihalyi, Mihaly. 1999. Implications of a systems perspective for the study of creativity. In *Handbook of Creativity*, edited by Robert J. Sternberg, 313–35. Cambridge: Cambridge University Press.
Cunningham, Stuart. 2009. Trojan horse or Rorschach blot? Creative industries discourse around the world. *International Journal of Cultural Policy* 15 (4): 375–86. doi: 10.1080/10286630902977501.

Dalsgaard, Peter. 2014. Pragmatism and design thinking. *International Journal of Design* 8 (1).
Dalton, Benjamin. 2004. Creativity, habit, and the social products of creative action: Revising Joas, incorporating Bourdieu. *Sociological Theory* 22: 603–22. doi: 10.1111/j.0735-2751.2004.00236.x.
Davis, Howard, and Richard Scase. 2000. *Managing creativity: The dynamics of work and organization, Managing work and organizations series*. Buckingham: Open University Press.
Dawson, Andrew, and Sean P. Holmes. 2012. *Working in the global film and television industries: Creativity, systems, space, patronage*. London: Bloomsbury Academic.
DCMS. 1998. *Creative industries: Mapping document*. London: Department for Culture, Media and Sport.
Deuze, Mark. 2019. On creativity. *Journalism* 20 (1): 130–34. doi: 10.1177/1464884918807066.
Dewey, John. 1916. *Democracy and education: An introduction to the philosophy of education, Text-book series*. New York: Macmillan.
Dewey, John. 1934/1958. *Art as experience; 1*. New York: Capricorn.
DiMaggio, Paul, and Paul M. Hirsch. 1976. Production organizations in the arts. *American Behavioral Scientist* 19 (6): 735–52. doi: 10.1177/000276427601900605.
Dornfeld, Barry. 1998. *Producing public television, producing public culture*. Princeton, NJ: Princeton University Press.
Doyle, Gillian. 2013. *Understanding media economics*. 2nd ed. Los Angeles, CA: Sage.
Draper, Jimmy. 2014. Theorizing creative agency through "discerned savvy": A tool for the critical study of media industries. *Media, Culture & Society* 36 (8): 1118–33.
Duffy, Brooke Erin. 2015. The romance of work: Gender and aspirational labour in the digital culture industries. *International Journal of Cultural Studies* 19 (4): 441–57. doi: 10.1177/1367877915572186.
Eisenberger, Robert, and Linda Shanock. 2003. Rewards, intrinsic motivation, and creativity: A case study of conceptual and methodological isolation. *Creativity Research Journal* 15 (2–3): 121–30. doi: 10.1207/S15326934CRJ152&3_02.
Elster, Jon. 2000. *Ulysses unbound: Studies in rationality, precommitment, and constraints*. Cambridge: Cambridge University Press.
Falzon, Mark-Anthony. 2009. *Multi-sited ethnography: Theory, praxis and locality in contemporary research*. Farnham, UK: Ashgate.
Fill, Chris, Graham Hughes, and Scott De Francesco. 2013. *Advertising: Strategy, creativity and media*. Harlow: Pearson Education.
Foucault, Michel, ed. 2015. *Udvalgte forelæsninger og essays*. 1st ed. Brabrand: Reflect.
Frandsen, Kirsten. 2007. Produktionsanalyse: Teoretiske og metodiske problemstillinger. In *Tv-produktion—nye vilkår*, edited by Kirsten Frandsen and Hanne Bruun, 23–54. Frederiksberg: Samfundslitteratur.
From, Unni, and Nete Nørgaard Kristensen. 2014. Blockbusters as vehicles for cultural debate in cultural journalism. *Akademisk* Kvarter, Vol. 7.
Fulton, Janet Michelle. 2011. *Making the news: Print journalism and the creative process*. Newcastle, UK: University of Newcastle.

Gans, Herbert J. 1980. *Deciding what's news: A study of CBS evening news, NBC nightly news,* Newsweek, *and* Time. New York: Vintage Books.

Gardner, Howard. 1985. *Frames of mind: The theory of multiple intelligences.* New York: Basic Books.

Gardner, Howard. 1993. *Creating minds: An anatomy of creativity seen through the lives of Freud, Einstein, Picasso, Stravinsky, Eliot, Graham and Gandhi.* New York: Basic Books.

Gauntlett, David. 2015. *Making media studies: The creativity turn in media and communications studies* (Digital formations, 93). New York: Peter Lang.

Geertz, Clifford. 1975. *The interpretation of cultures.* London: Hutchinson.

Getzels, Jacob W., and Mihaly Csikszentmihalyi. 1976. *The creative vision: A longitudinal study of problem finding in art.* New York: John Wiley.

Gill, Rosalind, and Andy Pratt. 2008. In the social factory? Immaterial labour, precariousness and cultural work. *Theory, Culture & Society* 25 (7–8): 1–30. doi: 10.1177/0263276408097794.

Gitlin, Todd. 1983. *Inside prime time.* New York: Pantheon.

Glăveanu, Vlad P. 2020. A sociocultural theory of creativity: Bridging the social, the material, and the psychological. *Review of General Psychology* 24 (4): 335–54. doi: 10.1177/1089268020961763.

Glăveanu, Vlad Petre. 2013. Rewriting the language of creativity: The five A's framework. *Review of General Psychology* 17 (1): 69–81. doi: 10.1037/a0029528.

Grindstaff, Laura. 2002. *The money shot: Trash, class, and the making of TV talk shows.* Chicago: University of Chicago Press.

Gripsrud, Jostein. 1995. *The dynasty years: Hollywood television and critical media studies* (Comedia). London: Routledge.

Guilford, J. P. 1950. Creativity. *American Psychologist* 5 (9): 444–54. doi: 10.1037/h0063487.

Hammersley, Martyn, and Paul Atkinson. 1995. *Ethnography: Principles in practice.* 2nd ed. London: Routledge.

Hammett-Jamart, Julia, Petar Mitric, and Eva Novrup Redvall. 2019. *European film and television co-production: Policy and practice, palgrave European film and media studies.* Cham, Switzerland: Springer International Publishing AG.

Harder, Lars, and Rasmus Ladefoged. 2007. Programkonceptet i udviklingsfasen af dansk tv-produktion. In *Tv-produktion—nye vilkår*, edited by Kirsten Frandsen and Hanne Bruun, 111–32.

Hassall Thomsen, Line. 2013. *New struggles, old ideals: the everyday struggle towards being a "Good Journalist" inside public service TV newsrooms in the UK and Denmark.* Aarhus: Department of Aesthetic and Communication, Aarhus University.

Havens, Timothy. 2018. Production. In *The craft of criticism: Critical media studies in practice*, edited by Michael Kackman and Mary Celeste Kearney, 268–78. New York: Routledge.

Havens, Timothy, and Amanda D. Lotz. 2016. *Understanding media industries.* Oxford: Oxford University Press.

Hearn, Alison, and Stephanie Schoenhoff. 2015. From celebrity to influencer: Tracing the diffusion of celebrity value across the data stream. In *A Companion to Celebrity*, edited by P. David Marshall and Sean Redmond, 194–212. Hoboken, NJ: John Wiley & Sons, Inc.

Hennessey, Beth A., and Teresa M. Amabile. 2010. Creativity. *Annual Review of Psychology* 61 (1): 569–98. doi: 10.1146/annurev.psych.093008.100416.

Herbert, Daniel, Amanda D. Lotz, and Lee Marshall. 2019. Approaching media industries comparatively: A case study of streaming. *International Journal of Cultural Studies* 22 (3): 349–66. doi: 10.1177/1367877918813245.

Hesmondhalgh, David. 2013. *The cultural industries*. 3rd ed. London: SAGE.

Hesmondhalgh, David. 2019. *The cultural industries*. 4th ed. Los Angeles: SAGE.

Hesmondhalgh, David, and Sarah Baker. 2011. *Creative labour: Media work in three cultural industries, culture, economy and the social*. London: Routledge.

Hjarvard, Stig. 2016. *Medialisering: Mediernes rolle i social og kultural forandring*. Edited by Stig Hjarvard. 1st ed. Kbh: Hans Reitzel.

Holt, Jennifer, and Alisa Perren. 2009. *Media industries: History, theory, and method*. Oxford: Wiley-Blackwell.

Inie, Nanna, and Peter Dalsgaard. 2017. A typology of design ideas. Proceedings of the 2017 ACM SIGCHI Conference on Creativity and Cognition, Singapore.

Jensen, Pia Majbritt. 2018. Far away, so close: Sydney-siders watching Forbrydelsen, Borgen and Bron/Broen. In *The Scandinavian Invasion*, edited by Richard McCulloch and William Proctor. Bern, Switzerland: Peter Lang.

Jerslev, Anne. 2014. *Reality-tv, Kort og præcist om medier og kommunikation*. Frederiksberg: Samfundslitteratur.

John-Steiner, Vera. 2000. *Creative collaboration*. Oxford: Oxford University Press.

Jones, Candace, Mark Lorenzen, and Jonathan Sapsed. 2015. Creative industries: A typology of change. In *The Oxford Handbook of Creative Industries*, edited by Candace Jones, Mark Lorenzen, and Jonathan Sapsed. Oxford: Oxford University Press.

Karppinen, Kari, and Hallvard Moe. 2011. What we talk about when we talk about document analysis. In *Trends in Communication Policy Research: New Theories, Methods and Subjects*, edited by Manuel Puppis and Natascha Just. Bristol: Intellect.

Kaufman, James C., and Robert J. Sternberg. 2010. *The Cambridge handbook of creativity* (Cambridge Handbooks in Psychology). New York: Cambridge University Press.

Kellner, Douglas. 2009. Media industries, political economy, and media/cultural studies. In *Media Industries: History, Theory, and Method*, edited by Jennifer Holt and Alisa Perren, 95–107. Oxford: Wiley-Blackwell.

Kerr, Aphra. 2017. *Global games: Production, circulation and policy in the networked era*. New York: Routledge.

Kerrigan, Susan. 2013. Accommodating creative documentary practice within a revised systems model of creativity. *Journal of Media Practice* 14 (2): 111–27. doi: 10.1386/jmpr.14.2.111_1.

Klausen, Søren Harnow. 2010. The notion of creativity revisited: A philosophical perspective on creativity research. *Creativity Research Journal* 22 (4): 347–60. doi: 10.1080/10400419.2010.523390.

Komorowski, Marlen, and Ike Picone. 2020. *Creative cluster development: Governance, place-making and entrepreneurship, regions and cities*. Milton, UK: Taylor and Francis.

Koskinen, Ilpo Kalevi. 2011. *Design research through practice: From the lab, field, and showroom*. Waltham, MA: Morgan Kaufmann.

Kozinets, Robert V. 2012. *Netnography: Doing ethnographic research online*. Los Angeles: Sage.

Kuehn, Kathleen, and Thomas F. Corrigan. 2013. Hope labor: The role of employment prospects in online social production. *The Political Economy of Communication* 1 (1): 9–25.

Küng, Lucy. 2008. *Strategic management in the media: From theory to practice*. Los Angeles: Sage.

Kvale, Steinar, and Svend Brinkmann. 2015. *Interview: det kvalitative forskningsinterview som håndværk [Interview: the qualitative research interview as a craft]*. 3rd ed. Copenhagen: Hans Reitzel.

Laclau, Ernesto, and Chantal Mouffe. 2001. *Hegemony and socialist strategy: Towards a radical democratic politics*. 2nd ed. London: Verso.

Lee, David. 2012. Precarious creativity: Changing attitudes towards craft and creativity in the British independent television production sector. *Creative Industries Journal* 4 (2): 155–70. doi: 10.1386/cij.4.2.155_1.

Lewin, Kurt. 1943. Defining the "field at a given time." *Psychological Review* 50 (3): 292–310. doi: 10.1037/h0062738.

Li, Vivian, Alex Shaw, and Kristina R. Olson. 2013. Ideas versus labor: What do children value in artistic creation? *Cognition* 127 (1): 38–45. doi: doi.org/10.1016/j.cognition.2012.11.001.

Lubart, Todd, and Maud Besançon. 2017. On the measurement and mismeasurement of creativity. In *Creative Contradictions in Education: Cross Disciplinary Paradoxes and Perspectives*, edited by Ronald A. Beghetto and Bharath Sriraman, 333–48. Cham, Switzerland: Springer International Publishing.

Luckman, Susan, and Stephanie Taylor. 2018. *The new normal of working lives: Critical studies in contemporary work and employment, dynamics of virtual work*. Cham, Switzerland: Springer International Publishing.

Marcus, George E. 1995. Ethnography in/of the world system: The emergence of multi-sited ethnography. *Annual Review of Anthropology* 24 (1): 95–117. doi: 10.1146/annurev.an.24.100195.000523.

Markman, Kris M. 2012. Doing radio, making friends, and having fun: Exploring the motivations of independent audio podcasters. *New Media & Society* 14 (4): 547–65. doi: 10.1177/1461444811420848.

Mayer, Vicki. 2008. Studying up and f**cking up: Ethnographic interviewing in production studies. *Cinema Journal* 47 (2): 141–48.

Mayer, Vicki. 2011. *Below the line: Producers and production studies in the new television economy*. Durham, NC: Duke University Press.

Mayer, Vicki. 2013. Cast-aways: The plights and pleasures of reality casting and production studies. In *A Companion to Reality Television*, edited by Laurie Ouellette, 57–73. Hoboken, NJ: John Wiley & Sons, Inc.

Mayer, Vicki, Miranda J. Banks, and John Thornton Caldwell. 2009. *Production studies: Cultural studies of media industries*. New York: Routledge.

McCabe, Janet, and Kim Akass. 2007. *Quality TV: Contemporary American television and beyond*. London: I. B. Tauris.

McIntyre, Phillip. 2012. *Creativity and cultural production: Issues for media practice*. Basingstoke, UK: Palgrave Macmillan.

McIntyre, Phillip, Janet Fulton, and Elizabeth Paton. 2016. *The creative system in action: Understanding cultural production and practice*. Houndmills, Basingstoke, Hampshire, UK: Palgrave Macmillan.

McRobbie, Angela. 1998. *British fashion design: Rag trade or image industry?* London: Routledge.

McRobbie, Angela. 2002. Clubs to companies: Notes on the decline of political culture in speeded up creative worlds. *Cultural Studies* 16 (4): 516–31. doi: 10.1080/09502380210139098.

McRobbie, Angela. 2016. *Be creative: Making a living in the new culture industries*. Cambridge: Polity Press.

Miège, Bernard. 1989. *The capitalization of cultural production*. New York: International General.

Mockros, Carol A., and Mihaly Csikszentmihalyi. 2014. The social construction of creative lives. In *The Systems Model of Creativity: The Collected Works of Mihaly Csikszentmihalyi*, 127–60. Dordrecht: Springer Netherlands.

Moeran, Brian, and Bo T. Christensen. 2013. *Exploring creativity: Evaluative practices in innovation, design and the arts*. Cambridge: Cambridge University Press.

Morgan, George, and Pariece Nelligan. 2015. Labile labour—gender, flexibility and creative work. *The Sociological Review* 63 (S1): 66–83. doi: 10.1111/1467-954X.12241.

Negus, Keith. 2002. The work of cultural intermediaries and the enduring distance between production and consumption. *Cultural Studies* 16 (4): 501–15. doi: 10.1080/09502380210139089.

Negus, Keith, and Michael Pickering. 2004. *Creativity, communication, and culture value*. London: SAGE.

Newcomb, Horace, and Robert S. Alley. 1983. *The producer's medium: Conversations with creators of American TV*. New York: Oxford University Press.

Newcomb, Horace, and Amanda Lotz. 2002. The production of media fiction. In *A Handbook of Media and Communication Research. Qualitative and Quantitative Methodologies*, edited by Klaus Bruhn Jensen, 62–77. London & New York: Routledge.

Nylund, Mats. 2013. Toward creativity management: Idea generation and newsroom meetings. *The International Journal on Media Management* 15 (4): 197–210. doi: 10.1080/14241277.2013.773332.

Olson, Scott Robert. 1999. *Hollywood planet: Global media and the competitive advantage of narrative transparency* (LEA's communication series). Mahwah, NJ: Lawrence Erlbaum.

Osborn, Alex F. 1953/1963. *Applied imagination: Principles and procedures of creative problem-solving*. 3. rev. ed. New York.
Owen, Charles. 1993. Considering design fundamentally. *Design Processes Newsletter* 5 (3).
Ozimek, Anna Maria. 2018. *Videogame work in Poland. Investigating creative labour in a post-socialist cultural industry* [PhD thesis]. University of Leeds.
Paterson, Chris, and David Domingo. 2008. *Making online news, Vol. 1: The ethnography of new media production*. New York: Peter Lang.
Paterson, Chris, David Lee, Anamik Saha, and Anna Zoellner. 2016. *Advancing media production research: Shifting sites, methods, and politics, global transformations in media and communication research*. Basingstoke, UK: Palgrave Macmillan.
Paulus, Paul B., and Bernard Arjan Nijstad. 2003. *Group creativity: Innovation through collaboration*. New York: Oxford University Press.
Pink, Sarah. 2016. *Digital ethnography: Principles and practice*. London: SAGE Publications Ltd.
Pjajčíková, Eva, and Petr Szczepanik. 2015. Group writing for post-socialist television. In *Production studies, the sequel!: Cultural studies of global media industries*, edited by Miranda J. Banks, Bridget Conor, and Vicki Mayer. New York: Routledge.
Pokorny, Michael, and John Sedgwick. 2010. Profitability trends in Hollywood, 1929 to 1999: somebody must know something. *Economic History Review* 63 (1): 56–84. doi: 10.1111/j.1468-0289.2009.00488.x.
Polanyi, Michael. 1967. *The tacit dimension*. London: Routledge & Kegan Paul.
Powdermaker, Hortense. 1950. *Hollywood: The dream factory: An anthropologist looks at the movie-makers*. Boston: Little, Brown.
Puijk, Roel. 2008. Ethnographic media production research in a digital environment. In *Making Online News*, edited by Chris Paterson and David Domingo. New York: Peter Lang.
Puijk, Roel. 2016. Forskning på produksjon av levende bilder. In *Bak kamera: norsk film og TV i et produksjonsperspektiv*, edited by Eva Bakøy, Tore Helseth, and Roel Puijk, 224 s., illustreret. Vallset: Oplandske bokforlag.
Reckwitz, Andreas. 2017. *The invention of creativity: Modern society and the culture of the new*. Cambridge: Polity Press.
Redvall, Eva Novrup. 2010. *Manuskriptskrivning som kreativ proces: de kreative samarbejder bag manuskriptskrivning i dansk spillefilm: ph.d.-afhandling*. Copenhagen: Institut for Medier, Erkendelse og Formidling, Københavns Universitet.
Redvall, Eva Novrup. 2014. *Writing and producing television drama in Denmark: From "The Kingdom" to "The Killing"* (Palgrave studies in screenwriting). Houndmills, Basingstoke, UK: Palgrave Macmillan.
Redvall, Eva Novrup, and Hanne Bruun. 2022. *Medieproduktionsanalyse*. 1st ed., *Kort og præcist om medier og kommunikation*. Frederiksberg: Samfundslitteratur.
Rhodes, Mel. 1961. An analysis of creativity. *The Phi Delta Kappan* 42 (7): 305–10.
Roberts, James Paul. 2010. Revisiting the creative/commercial clash: An analysis of decision-making during product development in the television industry. *Media, Culture & Society* 32 (5): 761–80. doi: 10.1177/0163443710373952.

Roberts, Sarah T. 2019. *Behind the screen: Content moderation in the shadows of social media*. New Haven, CT: Yale University Press.

Ross, Andrew. 2008. The new geography of work: Power to the precarious? *Theory, Culture & Society* 25 (7–8): 31–49. doi: 10.1177/0263276408097795.

Runco, Mark A., and Garrett J. Jaeger. 2012. The standard definition of creativity. *Creativity Research Journal* 24 (1): 92. doi: 10.1080/10400419.2012.650092.

Runco, Mark A., Garnet Millar, Selcuk Acar, and Bonnie Cramond. 2010. Torrance tests of creative thinking as predictors of personal and public achievement: A fifty-year follow-up. *Creativity Research Journal* 22 (4): 361–68. doi: 10.1080/10400419.2010.523393.

Ryan, Bill. 1991. *Making capital from culture, the corporate form of capitalist cultural production*. Berlin/Boston: De Gruyter.

Ryfe, David M. 2016. The importance of time in media production research. In *Advancing Media Production Research: Shifting Sites, Methods, and Politics*, edited by Chris Paterson, David Lee, Anamik Saha, and Anna Zoellner, 38–50. Basingstoke, UK: Palgrave Macmillan.

Saha, Anamik. 2017. *Race and the cultural industries*. Malden, MA: Polity Press.

Sarris, Andrew. 1963. The auteur theory. *Film Quarterly* 16 (4): 26–33.

Sawyer, Keith. 2003. *Group creativity: Music, theater, collaboration*. Mahwah, NJ: L. Erlbaum Associates.

Sawyer, Keith. 2012. *Explaining creativity: The science of human innovation*. 2nd ed. New York: Oxford University Press.

Sawyer, Keith. 2013. Evaluative practices in the creative industries. In *Exploring Creativity: Evaluative Practices in Innovation, Design and the Arts*, edited by Brian Moeran and Bo T. Christensen, 278–304. Cambridge: Cambridge University Press.

Sawyer, Keith, and Stacy DeZutter. 2009. Distributed creativity: How collective creations emerge from collaboration. *Psychology of Aesthetics, Creativity, and the Arts* 3 (2): 81–92. doi: 10.1037/a0013282.

Schein, Edgar H. 1985. *Organizational culture and leadership*. 2nd ed. San Francisco: Jossey-Bass Publishers.

Schlesinger, Philip. 1979. *Putting "reality" together: BBC news*. Repr. ed., Communication and Society; 9. London: Constable.

Schlesinger, Philip. 2007. Creativity: From discourse to doctrine? *Screen* XLVIII (3): 377.

Schlesinger, Philip. 2010. "The most creative organization in the world"? The BBC, "creativity" and managerial style. *International Journal of Cultural Policy* 16 (3): 271–85. doi: 10.1080/10286630903302766.

Schön, Donald A. 1983. *The reflective practitioner: How professionals think in action*. New York: Basic Books.

Schön, Donald A. 1992. Designing as reflective conversation with the materials of a design situation. *Research in Engineering Design* 3 (3): 131–47. doi: 10.1007/bf01580516.

Sherman, Zoe. 2020. *Modern advertising and the market for audience attention: The US advertising industry's turn-of-the-twentieth-century transition* (Routledge explorations in economic history). Abingdon, Oxon: Routledge.

Shoemaker, Pamela J. 1991. *Gatekeeping, communication concepts; 3.* Newbury Park, CA: Sage.
Shoemaker, Pamela J., and Tim P. Vos. 2009. *Gatekeeping theory.* London: Routledge.
Simmel, Georg. 1978. *The philosophy of money.* London: Routledge & Kegan Paul.
Sotamaa, Olli, and Jan Švelch. 2021. *Game production studies.* Amsterdam University Press.
Spicer, Andrew, and Steve Presence. 2017. *Go West! Bristol's film and television industries.* Bristol: University of the West of England.
Spinelli, Martin, and Lance Dann. 2019. *Podcasting: The audio media revolution.* 1st ed. London: Bloomsbury Publishing Plc.
Staiger, Janet. 2003. Authorship approaches. In *Authorship and Film*, edited by David A. Gerstner and Janet Staiger, 308. New York: Routledge.
Stake, Robert E. 2005. Qualitative case studies. In *The Sage Handbook of Qualitative Research*, edited by Norman K. Denzin and Yvonna S. Lincoln, 443–66. Thousand Oaks, CA: Sage Publications.
Stein, Morris I. 1953. Creativity and culture. *The Journal of Psychology* 36 (2): 311–22. doi: 10.1080/00223980.1953.9712897.
Stephensen, Jan Løhmann. 2018. *Kreativitet, Tænkepauser; 61.* [Aarhus]: Aarhus Universitetsforlag.
Sternberg, Robert J., and Linda A. O'Hara. 1998. Creativity and intelligence. In *Handbook of Creativity*, edited by Robert J. Sternberg, 251–72. Cambridge: Cambridge University Press.
Stokes, Patricia D. 2006. *Creativity from constraints: The psychology of breakthrough.* New York: Springer Pub. Co.
Sundet, Vilde Schanke. 2021a. Provocation: Why I want to talk television with global platform representatives. *Critical Studies in Television.* doi: 10.1177/17496020211044918.
Sundet, Vilde Schanke. 2021b. *Television drama in the age of streaming: Transnational strategies and digital production cultures at the NRK.* Cham: Springer International Publishing AG.
Sundet, Vilde Schanke, and Terje Colbjørnsen. 2021. Streaming across industries: Streaming logics and streaming lore across the music, film, television, and book industries. *MedieKultur: Journal of Media and Communication Research* 37 (70): 12–31. doi: 10.7146/mediekultur.v37i70.122425.
Syvertsen, Trine. 1997. *Den store TV-krigen: norsk allmennfjernsyn 1988–96.* Bergen-Sandviken: Fagbokforl.
Szczepanik, Petr, and Patrick Vonderau. 2013. *Behind the screen: Inside European production cultures, global cinema.* New York: Palgrave Macmillan.
Tanggaard, Lene. 2015. The creative pathways of everyday life. *The Journal of Creative Behavior* 49 (3): 181–93. doi: 10.1002/jocb.95.
Taylor, Stephanie. 2012. The meanings and problems of contemporary creative work. *Studies in Vocational and Professional Education* 5 (1): 41–57. doi: 10.1007/s12186-011-9065-6.

Taylor, Stephanie. 2013. The lived experience of a contemporary creative identification. In *Handbook of Research on Creativity*, edited by Janet Chan and Kerry Thomas, 175–84. Cheltenham: Edward Elgar Publishing Ltd.

Taylor, Stephanie. 2015. A new mystique? Working for yourself in the neoliberal economy. *The Sociological Review (Keele)* 63 (S1): 174–87. doi: 10.1111/1467-954X.12248.

Taylor, Stephanie, and Karen Littleton. 2012. *Contemporary identities of creativity and creative work*. Farnham: Ashgate.

Taylor, Stephanie, and Susan Luckman. 2020. *Pathways into creative working lives, the creative workshop series*. Cham: Springer International Publishing AG.

Thimm, Caja, Mario Anastasiadis, and Jessica Einspänner-Pflock. 2018. *Media logic(s) revisited: modelling the interplay between media institutions, media technology and societal change, transforming communications*. Cham: Springer International Publishing AG.

Thomas, Gary. 2015. *How to do your case study*. 2nd ed. London: SAGE.

Toynbee, Jason. 2000. *Making popular music: Musicians, creativity and institutions*. London: Arnold.

Ursell, Gillian. 2000. Television production: Issues of exploitation, commodification and subjectivity in UK television labour markets. *Media, Culture & Society* 22 (6): 805–25. doi: 10.1177/016344300022006006.

Valsiner, Jaan, and Alberto Rosa. 2007. *The Cambridge handbook of sociocultural psychology* (Cambridge handbooks in psychology). Cambridge: Cambridge University Press.

Van den Bulck, Hilde, Manuel Puppis, Karen Donders, and Leo Van Audenhove. 2019. *The Palgrave handbook of methods for media policy research*. Cham: Springer International Publishing AG.

van Dijck, José, Thomas Poell, and Martijn de Waal. 2018. *The platform society*. New York: Oxford University Press.

van Keulen, Jolien. 2021. Following the recipe: Producing *The Great British Bake Off* in Flanders. *Critical Studies in Television* 16 (3): 286–303. doi: 10.1177/17496020211020312.

Van Maanen, John. 1979. The fact of fiction in organizational ethnography. *Administrative Science Quarterly* 24 (4): 539–50. doi: 10.2307/2392360.

Vaughan, Laurene. 2017. *Practice-based design research*. London: Bloomsbury Academic.

Weisberg, Robert W. 1993. *Creativity: Beyond the myth of genius* (a series of books in psychology). New York: W.H. Freeman.

Westmeyer, Hans. 1998. The social construction and psychological assessment of creativity. *High Ability Studies* 9 (1): 11–21. doi: 10.1080/1359813980090102.

White, David Manning. 1950. The gate keeper: A case study in the selection of news. *Journalism Quarterly* 27 (4): 383.

Willig, Ida. 2011. *Bag nyhederne: Værdier, idealer og praksis*. 2nd ed. Frederiksberg: Samfundslitteratur.

Wolff, Janet. 1981. *The social production of art, communications and culture*. London: Macmillan.

Wollen, Peter. 1972. The auteur theory. In *Film Theory and Criticism: Introductory Readings*, edited by Leo Braudy and Marshall Cohen, 905. New York: Oxford University Press.

Wright, David. 2018. *"Hopeful work" and the creative economy.* Cham, Switzerland: Springer International Publishing.

Wyatt, Wendy N., and Kristie Bunton. 2012. *The ethics of reality TV: A philosophical examination.* New York: Bloomsbury Academic & Professional.

Ytreberg, Espen. 2000. Tekstproduksjonsstudier som medievitenskapelig forskningsområde [Text production studies as a media studies research area]. *Nordicom Information* (2): 51–60.

Zoellner, Anna. 2015. Detachment, pride, critique—Professional identity in independant factual television production in Great Britain and Germany. In *Production Studies, the Sequel!: Cultural Studies of Global Media Industries*, edited by Miranda J. Banks, Bridget Conor, and Vicki Mayer, 150–63. New York: Routledge.

Index

access, 45, 48–49, 57
advertising, 33, 36, 40, 64, 71, 85–86
agency. *See* autonomy
artistic approach, 3–4, 10, 21–28, 33, 35–36, 66, 68–71
assessment. *See* creative evaluations
audience, 14, 28, 31, 33–36, 39, 41, 60, 78, 81, 87
authorship, 3, 10, 22–23, 34, 55, 70
autonomy, 5–6, 25, 31, 33–37, 41, 83

brainstorming. *See* idea development
briefs, 39–40, 76–80

case studies, 41, 54, 59, 66, 73, 81
case example, 75–81, 84
collectivist approach, 17–19, 54, 67
constraints, 5, 19–20, 26, 33–35, 40, 50, 60, 67, 76, 78, 80, 87
creative: awareness, 56–57, 61, 67–68, 75, 78, 84, 87–88; evaluations, 2, 5–6, 28, 37–38, 41–42, 57, 61, 65; expectations, 5, 19, 42, 58, 71–72, 77–80, 87–88; industries, 3–5, 10, 16, 19, 21–28, 35–37, 42, 66, 68–69, 88; processes, 2, 5–7, 12–15, 17–23, 26, 29, 31, 35, 40–43, 54, 60, 64–77, 80–81, 84–88; value, 15, 29, 38, 42, 47, 54, 66–67, 81; workers, 1, 25, 27–28, 36, 57, 67–69, 72. *See* creative workers
creativity: everyday, 1–5, 16, 18, 26, 40, 54–55; research, 1–7, 9–17, 28, 32–35, 37, 83, 85, 87; sociocultural, 2, 12–17, 28, 42, 54, 65–66; *See* creativity research; negative approach
cultural industries. *See* creative industries
cultural production. *See* cultural products, cultural studies
cultural products, 10, 16, 21–23, 26, 31, 41, 47
cultural studies, 3–5, 21–24, 32–34, 46–47

design studies, 10, 18–27, 34, 38, 67
developers, 5, 39–42, 71, 76–80
disappointment. *See* failure
document analysis, 45, 69
domain, 12, 14–15, 39, 86

editors, 36, 39–41, 65, 68, 75–81, 88
ethnography. *See* observations
evaluations. *See* creative evaluations
exclusive informants. *See* informants

failure, 6, 35–37, 43, 72–73, 80, 87

fieldwork, 19, 40, 58, 75, 80
film: industry, 23, 37, 45; production, 55, 72; studies, 3, 22–23
five traditions in creativity research, 2, 4, 9, 15, 29–30, 32, 38, 63, 67–68, 72–73, 81, 83

gaming. *See* video game industry
gate keeping, 14–15, 37–38, 40–43, 57, 65–66, 76, 79, 84
genres. *See* media genres
group processes, 18, 21

humanities. *See* artistic approach

idea development, 11, 29, 37–41, 51, 55, 58, 75–78, 80, 85
individualist approach, 10–13, 16–18, 22, 59, 63–65
informants, 19, 27–28, 41, 49, 56–59, 70–72, 88
innovation, 11, 15, 24, 36, 84
intentional overproduction, 36
interviews, 24, 27, 34, 39, 45, 56–59, 64, 66, 69, 73, 75, 78

journalism, 17, 32, 39–41, 46, 50, 67, 72, 78, 86

management. *See* media management
media: content, 3, 31, 33–34, 36, 41, 45, 55, 60–61, 64–65, 72, 75, 81, 85–88; economy, 23, 34–37; genres, 34, 42, 48, 50, 60–61, 64, 76, 86–87; industries, 2–5, 15–16, 18–21, 29, 31–42, 45–50, 53, 55, 57, 59–61, 63–74, 80–81, 83–88; logics, 60; management, 18, 20–21, 34, 39–41, 46, 65–68, 76, 86; organizations, 11, 14–18, 21, 23, 28–29, 33–37, 39–41, 45–50, 54–59, 65–72, 84–88; production, 3, 15, 17, 32, 34–35, 39, 45–47, 50–51, 57, 64, 67, 69, 72, 84–85; studies, 1–4, 10, 31, 53, 64. *See* audience; creative workers

methods: qualitative, 49, 56, 58–59, 66, 73, 84; quantitative, 49, 53, 56, 59, 64, 73, 84
music industry, 3, 18, 23–25, 27, 32, 41, 86
myths, 10–12, 17, 22, 28, 34, 61, 71

negative approach, 5, 29, 56, 71, 73
nobody knows, 35–36, 43, 80

observations, 19, 34, 39, 45–46, 56–59, 64, 66, 69, 72, 75–79
organizations. *See* media organizations

participant observation. *See* observations
pitching ideas, 39–40, 42, 49–50, 55, 75–76, 78–79
podcast industry, 16, 36, 50, 64–65, 72, 85–86
political economy, 32, 46–47
pragmatic approach, 5, 10, 17–21, 26, 34–35, 37, 40, 66–69, 78
precarious. *See* working conditions
production. *See* media production
production studies, 3, 32, 45–51, 53, 56, 75, 86
professionals. *See* creative workers
psychology, 1–5, 9–17, 19–21, 27, 34, 38, 63–64, 72

radio industry, 3, 17, 23, 32, 60, 65, 67, 86
reality TV, 61, 87
research. *See* creativity research
research challenges, 46, 48–50, 53–61, 69–70, 73, 86
research design, 63–73
research methodology. *See* methods
researching creativity. *See* creativity research
risks, 35–37, 80, 84, 87
romantic understanding, 2, 4, 10, 12, 23–26, 40, 78, 84

self-reflexivity, 34, 47, 56

social constructivist, 10, 15, 27–29, 42, 54, 66, 71–73, 88
sociocultural psychology. *See* sociocultural creativity
social dynamics, 5, 13, 17, 40–42, 47, 49, 55, 57, 65–66, 72, 79, 81, 88
streaming, 33, 48, 81, 85
stress, 29, 80–81
sunk costs, 35, 81

television: fiction or factual programming, 50, 64, 81, 86; industry, 16, 23, 25, 34, 39, 60–61, 75–81, 87; studies, 85. *See* reality TV
texts. *See* media content
time (as a factor), 28, 38, 47–48, 50–51, 54, 58, 72–73, 78, 81, 84, 87

video game industry, 16–17, 25, 35, 38, 50, 55, 64–67, 70, 72, 85–88

working conditions, 4, 10, 20–21, 23–28, 33, 54, 68–70, 80, 88

About the Author

Mads Møller Tommerup Andersen is an assistant professor at University of Copenhagen. Since 2016, he has worked with the topic of creativity in media industries in order to find connections between creativity research and media studies. In 2019, he published his dissertation *DR3 and the Creative Pressure* about the creative processes and idea development at a Danish public-service youth TV channel. His research interests also include creative industries, streaming, TV production, media history, and media policy.

www.ingramcontent.com/pod-product-compliance
Lightning Source LLC
Chambersburg PA
CBHW020129010526
44115CB00008B/1042